A HANDBOOK FOR QUALITY PROFESSIONALS

Designing A World-Class Quality Management System For FDA Regulated Industries

Quality System Requirements (QSR) For cGMP

by

David N. Muchemu

authorHOUSE®

AuthorHouse™
1663 Liberty Drive, Suite 200
Bloomington, IN 47403
www.authorhouse.com
Phone: 1-800-839-8640

This book is a work of non-fiction. Unless otherwise noted, the author
and the publisher make no explicit guarantees as to the accuracy of

© 2008 David N. Muchemu. All rights reserved.

No part of this book may be reproduced, stored in a retrieval system, or
transmitted by any means without the written permission of the author.

First published by AuthorHouse 4/2/2008

ISBN: 978-1-4343-4871-5 (sc)
ISBN: 978-1-4343-4872-2 (hc)

Printed in the United States of America
Bloomington, Indiana

This book is printed on acid-free paper.

DEDICATION

This book is dedicated to all the teachers who made a difference in my life. At the top of the list is my brother, the late Mr. James Felix Wamoya of Elgon Estate Primary School in Turbo. Next are the following teachers from Kapsabet Boys High School: Mr. Thomas Amuhaya, my chemistry and biology teacher, who made science fun! Mr. Namwamba, my physics teacher, who made physics understandable and fun. The headmaster of Kapsabet Boys High School, Mr. Thomas K. Kimunai, who taught me the value of collective responsibility, hard work, and networking, and instilled in me the belief that I was destined for greater things. Sir, those lectures you gave during school supper about "opening new embassies" paid off! Next I would like to dedicate this book to Mr. David K. N'getich, the bursar of Kapsabet Boys High School and Mr. Omotto, the housemaster of Naivasha house during my tenure as house captain. Mr. Omotto taught me that leadership was about serving others first. Mr. N'getich taught me the value of organizational management. This book is also dedicated to professors and instructors at Warren Wilson College in Swannanoa, North Carolina, and professors at the University of New Mexico and JFK University in Walnut Creek, California. Thank you for introducing me to Peter Senge's systems approach to quality management. Finally, I would like to dedicate this book to all professionals who make quality products in the pharmaceutical, medical device, biomedical, and tissue industries. Your work improves the human condition around the world. Your effort is appreciated!

David N. Muchemu, CQE, MBA
Chief Executive Officer (CEO)
Quality Systems International (QSi) LLC
San Jose, California, USA
August 2007

Yet another cGMP product from:

QSi (LLC) is a member of the Silicon Valley (San Jose) chamber of commerce and

a member of the **San Jose B**etter **B**usiness **B**ureau.

Quality is everybody's job!™

About the Author

David N.Muchemu is the author of "How to Design A World-Class Corrective Action and Preventive Action System for FDA regulated industries",and "Change Control for FDA Regulated Industries". Mr Muchemu has extensive experience in Pharmaceutical,Medical Device,Biomedical,and Tissue Industries.He has worked in different capacities at Boston Scientific,Johnson and Johnson,American Redcross Biomedical services,Guidant,Advanced Bionics , Applied Biosystems and Tissue Banks International.He is the founder of QSi (LLC),a Quality Management System/cGMP consulting firm in San Jose,California.

Contents

CHAPTER ONE
Quality management system (QMS) defined. 1

CHAPTER TWO
Functions of quality subsystems 19

CHAPTER THREE:
Quality system regulations (QSR). 23

CHAPTER FOUR
Document hierarchy 29

CHAPTER FIVE:
Contents of a quality manual 33

CHAPTER SIX
Quality sub-system policies 53

CHAPTER SEVEN
Standard operating procedures 63

CHAPTER EIGHT
Work instructions (WIs) 71

CHAPTER NINE
Documents and records controls 79

CHAPTER TEN
Quality system lexicon and acronyms 87

CHAPTER ELEVEN
How the FDA audits quality systems. 103

Appendix A
Quality system warning letters. 109

Appendix B
Bibliography 115

PREFACE

This book is designed to achieve two goals: first to help quality-system professionals in startup medical device, tissue, biomedical, and pharmaceutical organizations design quality management systems that meet and exceed the quality system regulations, also known as the QSR. My second goal for writing this book is to help management in organizations with warning letters or consent decrees related to their quality management systems meet and exceed compliance requirements. It is my hope that I have achieved both goals.

David N. Muchemu, MBA, BSc
CEO QSi (LLC)
San Jose, CA
USA
October 2007

CHAPTER ONE
QUALITY MANAGEMENT SYSTEM (QMS) DEFINED

The QSR (quality system regulations) define a quality management system as follows:

"**The organizational structure, responsibilities, processes, procedures, and resources for implementing quality management.**"

Source: 21CFR820.39 (v)

On the other hand, ISO 8402 defines a quality management system as follows:

"**The organizational structure, processes, procedures, and resources needed to implement** *quality* **management.**"

Source: ISO8402: 1994

The two definitions are in harmony with each other. However, the QSR puts emphasis on **ownership** or **responsibilities**; hence the importance of the use of cross-functional process maps to show how work flows between departments. With any quality management system, there has to be ownership of the several cross-functional quality subsystems. And there are several cross-functional quality subsystems in any given quality management system. The QSR requires seven, the core of which is **management controls**. The seven recommended quality subsystems are discussed in later chapters. According to the QSR definition, any quality management system should have the following five elements:

1. ORGANIZATIONAL STRUCTURE

There has to be a documented structure in the form of an organization chart representing the leadership of the entire organization and detailing the different parts of the quality unit. In most organizations the quality unit is also referred to as the quality department. However, some organizations prefer to bring the quality unit under the umbrella of quality and regulatory affairs. The structure chosen should fit the culture of the organization.

2. RESPONSIBILITIES

Any quality system has to have established ownership of the different parts of the quality unit. Suggested ownership tittles are:
- Vice president of quality
- Quality manager
- Quality system manager
- Production manager
- Engineering manager
- Quality engineer
- Process engineer
- Supplier quality manager
- Supplier quality engineer
- Change control manager
- CAPA system administrator

These are suggestions. What titles you choose for your quality unit is entirely up to you. However, with every title come defined roles and responsibilities.

3. PROCESSES

A process by definition is a set of steps through which an input is converted into an output.

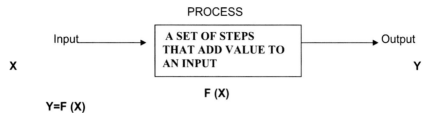

*Y happens when **F** adds value to any input **X** (equipment, work Instruction, personnel, and training, etc.).

Simply put, your organization has to have standardized steps by which tasks are accomplished. There has to be standard WORK INSTRUCTIONS that convert inputs (operator, material, machine, and environment) into predetermined outputs. The key here is to accomplish tasks the same way all the time using standardized procedures. Work instructions are the documents that answer the question **"How is this done?"** Work instructions are standardized step-by-step ways of accomplishing tasks with predetermined results. Results of a process are usually determined during process validation. The key here is that these documents are written in a first-person voice.

4. PROCEDURES

This requirement calls for STANDARD OPERATING PROCEDURES that accomplish work across functional groups. These are usually third-layer documents that describe ownership between departments. They layout **"who does what."** This set of documents is accompanied by a cross-functional map. They describe the order in which events unfold in the process map.

It is, therefore, good practice to draft a cross-functional map first before drafting a standard operating procedure. Standard operating procedures are usually written in second-person voice.

5. RESOURCES

Finally, your organization has to have enough qualified people to do the work that produces products that meet the requirements of your external customers. It is not enough just to have the numbers. Here is

a point that needs to be stressed: The quality of the personnel you hire matters. Your personnel have to be competent and trained for assigned jobs. Proof of their training has to be updated and maintained in training records. The second piece in the puzzle is infrastructure. The organization is required to have maintained infrastructure that achieves the external customers' requirements. Your specified infrastructure should include:
- Buildings
- Work space
- Utilities
- Equipment
- Transport system
- Communication system

Needless to say, what you choose to prioritize depends on the culture of your organization and the products and services your organization provides for external customers.

PARTS OF A QUALITY MANAGEMENT SYSTEM

The diagram below shows a model of a quality management system layout based on the ISO 9001 requirements. Unlike ISO 13485, which is required for all medical device companies, ISO 9001 is a voluntary quality management system and can be used as a model for any product. The only condition for this model is that you state your execution plan and you stick with it. In other words, say what you do and do what you say.

The so-called "elements" in the ISO quality system are what the FDA refers to as quality subsystems in the QSIT (quality system inspection technique) booklet. The QSIT focuses on **seven must-have** quality subsystems. The number of quality subsystems you choose for your organization should have at a minimum the seven subsystems that the FDA auditors focus on. At the top of the list are management controls.

David N. Muchemu

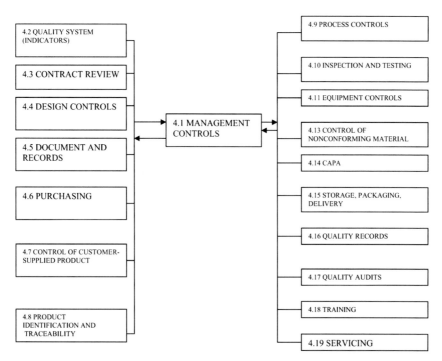

Management owns the quality system and is responsible for its health.

According to the quality management system regulations (QSR), management owns the quality management system of any organization; hence the importance of management review meetings led by a management representative. Management review meetings are held at specified times or periods to analyze data from different areas of the quality systems, especially the following data:

- CAPA
- Storage and distribution
- Quality system indicators
- Quality audits
- Training
- Service
- Purchasing
- Document control
- Quality system indicators
- Design controls
- Equipment controls
- Process controls

It is imperative for management to review data from the CAPA system for continuous process improvement. Most organizations are data rich, but collecting data for the sake of it is a waste of resources. Data on the quality management system should be collected for the sole purpose of continuous process improvement. The data that is collected should be used in combination with known facts to make good business decisions that can improve processes to deliver service or products that meet the requirements of external customers.

It should be noted here that whereas sections of the ISO quality subsystem are referred to as articles, my approach to the quality management system is "holistic." I take the approach that article 4.14 CAPA and article 4.9 Process controls are subsystems in a quality management system with ownership and outputs. For that reason, for the remainder of this book my discussion will be limited to systems and subsystems (thanks to Peter Senge!).

We have purposely chosen the ISO 9001 quality management model because ISO 13485 is a subset of ISO 9001. However, it should be stressed here that though ISO 13485 puts emphasis on the use of standardized processes, risk management, and customer involvement in continuous process improvement and the use of process maps, it is a required model for medical device companies. ISO 9001, on the other hand, is a voluntary standard that can be used for any quality management system.

MEDICAL DEVICE MODEL

The following medical device QMS model is based on the QSR model available on the FDA website. The model comprises the following quality subsystems:
- Design controls
- Production and process controls
- Records and documents
- Change controls
- Material controls
- Facilities and equipment controls
- CAPA
- Management controls

Each one of these subsystems has independent satellite feeder systems that accomplish given tasks. Here is a list of some of the subsystems and their satellite subsystems:

- **CAPA:** Is considered one of the most important quality subsystems, in that it monitors the health of the entire quality system. A CAPA subsystem is linked to the following satellite subsystems:

1. Removals and corrections
2. Reporting
3. Device tracking
4. Customer complaint subsystem
5. Servicing
6. Control of nonconforming products

- **Production and process controls:** Next to CAPA, this is properly the most important quality subsystem. It compiles real-time data from processes. It is linked to the following satellite subsystems:

1. Sterilization
2. Statistical process control
3. Process validation
4. Process validation
5. DHR
6. Equipment controls
7. Environmental controls
8. Facilities controls

- **Material controls:** Another important quality subsystem. It is linked to:

1. Acceptance activities
2. Material traceability
3. Material qualification
4. DHR
5. SCAR
6. Supplier qualification
7. Storage
8. Distribution
9. Nonconforming products

- **Change controls**: Some of the satellites for this quality subsystem include:

1. Manufacturing and process control
2. Document controls
3. Supplier management
4. Design controls
5. CAPA
6. Storage

- **Management controls:** This subsystem oversees all the satellites in the quality subsystem under the umbrella of "management review." By the QSR and ISO requirements the organization is required to appoint a management representative with authority to lead the periodic review process of the quality management subsystem for its suitability, maintenance, and effectiveness. A designated member of the management team with executive responsibility is also required to ensure the efficiency and adequacy of the quality management system. In most organizations, the authority of evaluating the quality system for its adequacy and efficiency rests with the vice president of quality. The management representative with authority is usually the quality manager, who reports to the vice president of quality. Several quality management models exist. Here are a few:

THE QSR BASED MODELS:

1. MEDICAL DEVICE

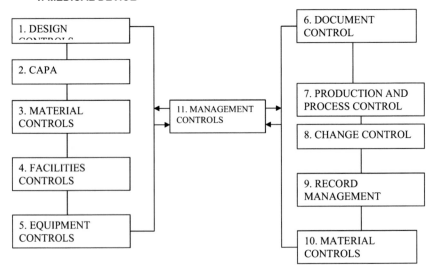

The QSR specifies **SEVEN** quality subsystems: design controls, material controls, record document and change controls, management controls, facilities and equipment controls, CAPA, and production and process controls. It is general practice to subdivide the seven recommended subsystems into eleven quality subsystems. The model above is **based** on the QSIT (quality systems inspection technique) model developed by the FDA's Office of Regulatory Affairs, and Center for Devices and Radiological Health. The above model comprises eleven quality subsystems, as opposed to the seven in the QSIT model. The belief here is that all quality subsystems do not operate in a vacuum. There is an interaction between processes in a quality subsystem to produce an output. Hence the process approach taken by ISO 13485 for a medical device quality management system. I should hasten to add that whatever quality system your organization designs, it should be one that is modeled around the organization's culture and one that the organization can stand behind during a regulatory audit. In other words (and I realize I am shooting myself in the foot!), you should never bring in a consultant to tell you what your quality management system should be. If anything, the consultant should only come in to work with the infrastructure and culture in place. There is no one shoe fits all when it comes to a quality management system.

2. THE ISO 13485 MODEL FOR MEDICAL DEVICES

Unlike ISO 9001, which has nineteen articles, ISO 13485 is reduced to eight articles. Quality systems requirements for ISO 13485 are specified in section 4.1. Subsystems are specified in articles 4.2 through article 8.5, entitled improvements.

The general requirement that stands out for this quality subsystem model is the "process approach" to quality management. In other words, you have to have processes in place to accomplish required tasks. Here are specified quality management system requirements:
- 4.0 QMS general requirements, (core quality system requirements)
- 5.0 Management controls
- 6.0 Resource management
- 7.0 Production and process controls (also known as" product realization")

- 8.0 Measurement and analysis (aka internal and external feedback loops)

4.0 QUALITY MANAGEMENT SYSTEM REQUIREMENTS

Your organization is required to meet the following general requirements:
- An established quality management system
- A documented quality management system
- Defined measures of success for the quality system
- Established processes
- Established process maps
- Defined process controls
- Resource availability and allocation
- Quality planning
- An implemented quality management system that achieves planned results
- A quality policy
- A quality manual
- Cross-functional documents
- Work instructions
- Records as proof of work done
- Job aids and other specified documents.

These items are covered in articles 4.1 through 4.2.2. Article 4.2.3 covers document control. Requirements for document control are:
- A documented process to review and approve documents before release
- A documented process for document changes, re-approvals, and updates
- A documented revision control process
- Identification of controlled and uncontrolled documents
- A documented process for document absolution

The next article, 4.2.4, addresses record management. Here are the requirements for records control:
- Records should be established and maintained to portray current state
- An established record-retention period policy
- Capability for easy retrieval of records
- An established standard operating procedure for the control, identification, storage, protection, and disposition of records
- Adherence to other specified local, national, and regional standards

5.0 MANAGEMENT CONTROLS (Management responsibility):

This article lays out requirements for the management team in a quality management system. It calls for the following requirements:
- Demonstrated commitment by management to develop, implement, and maintain an effective quality management system
- An established quality policy
- Established, planned, and measurable quality objectives
- Periodic quality review meetings resulting from audits, customer feedback, CAPA, change control, regulatory requirements, and supplier and customer change requests.
- Continuous review of the quality policy
- Controlled and planned changes to the quality management system
- Defined and documented authorities and responsibilities
- Appointment of a management representative by top management to oversee the quality management system
- Reports by management representatives to top management about the performance of the quality management system.
- Records of management review meetings

6.0 RESOURCE MANAGEMENT (Facilities and personnel)

This section combines personnel requirements and facilities requirements. The following are requirements for an effective quality management system:
- Competent personnel
- Training for personnel
- Personnel evaluation
- Personnel training records
- Adequate workspace
- Required equipment
- Established health, clothing, cleanliness, and environmental requirements

7.0 PRODUCT REALIZATION (Production and process controls, design controls, and materials controls)

This is the biggest section. It combines design controls, material controls, production and process controls; hence the name of the section: product realization.

The following are requirements for product realization in a quality management system:
- Established processes
- Established quality objectives
- Establish customer requirements
- Established criteria for acceptance
- Established process requirements through validation and verification
- Specified regulatory and statutory requirements
- Defined and documented product requirements
- Change control
- An established communication system between the customer and the organization
- Design review and design evaluation process
- Design verification process
- Product validation process
- Supplier selection, evaluation, approval, and qualification criteria
- Incoming material inspection
- Supplier control
- Product identification and traceability
- Equipment calibration process

8.0 MEASUREMENT, ANALYSIS, AND IMPROVEMENT

(Customer complaint subsystem, CAPA subsystem, audit subsystem, management review subsystem, material review subsystem)

This section covers part of the external and internal feedback loops. The section covers subsystems that tell the organization about its performance, internally and externally. Here are the specified requirements:
- Process performance measurement indicators
- Use of statistical techniques
- Customer satisfaction indicators
- Maintained audit system

- Specified quality indicators
- In-process inspection methods
- Maintained process records
- Nonconforming material control and disposition process
- Supplier performance indicators
- Use of trends for preventive action
- Use of change control for process and product improvement
- Documented procedures for the issue and implementation of advisory notices
- Documentation of customer complaints and investigations
- Investigation and elimination of nonconformities
- Investigation of potential nonconformities
- Documentation of all actions taken
- Review of all corrective actions taken for effectiveness

This section is the key to continuous process improvement. It puts emphasis on collection and analysis of data from two streams: the internal feedback loop that provides data from internal audits, process reviews, and CAPA; and the external feedback loop that collects data from external audits, third-party audits, and customer complaints.

2. ISO 13485 QMS LAYOUT

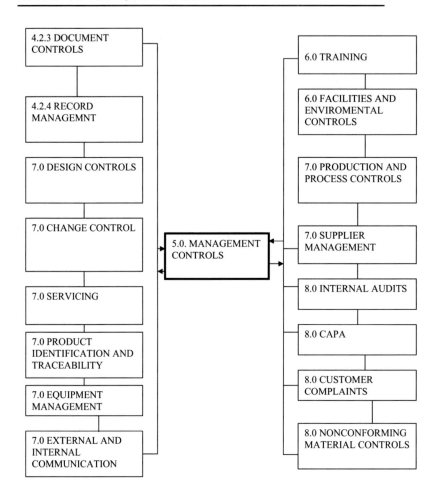

3. TISSUE AND CELLULAR THERAPY MODEL

This model is based on subpart D of current Good Tissue Practice (cGTP), established in 21CFR part 1271, which calls for the following requirements:

Section 1271.150 (a):
- Process steps for tissue recovery
- Process steps for donor screening
- Process steps for donor testing
- Process steps for donor processing

- Process steps for labeling
- Process steps for storage
- Process steps for packaging

Section 1271.160 (b), which calls for quality system functions:
- Established and maintained procedures
- Process for reviewing, approval, revising, and archiving procedures
- Corrective action and preventive action procedures
- Quality audit procedures
- Record management
- Deviation management
- Designated management representative over the quality program
- Management review

The elements or subsystems that comprise the quality management system are specified in sections 1271.170 through section 1271.320. They are:

1271.170 Management controls (organization and personnel)
1271.180 Document control (procedures)
1271.190 Facilities controls
1271.200 Equipment controls
1271.210 Supplies and reagents
1271.220 Process controls
1271.225 Change control (process changes)
1271.230 Process validation
1271.250 Labeling controls
1271.260 Storage
1271.265 Receipt and distribution
1271.270 Record management
1271.290 Product identification and traceability (tracking)
1271.320 Customer complaint system (complaint file)

SYSTEM LAYOUT:

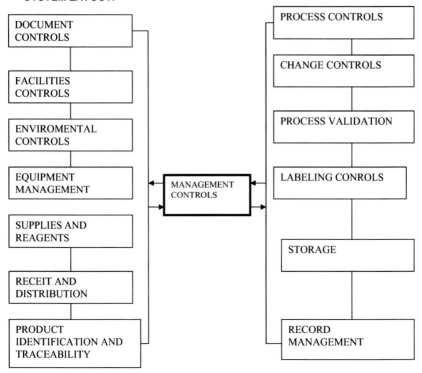

A cGTP quality system can be divided into thirteen quality subsystems, each with its own documentation hierarchy that may start from policy, standard operating procedures, work instructions, records, and job aids.

4. BIOMEDICAL AND PHARMACEUTICAL INDUSTRIES MODEL

The two groups are lumped together because of their similarities, whereas cGMPs for both drugs and biomedical products do not specify the quality system requirements. There are implied requirements for the quality management subsystem in both 21CFR part 210 and 21CFR part 606.

21 CFR 606, cGMPs for blood and blood components stipulates the following subparts or quality subsystems:
- Organization and personnel (management controls)
- Plant and facilities
- Equipment

- Production and process controls
- Finished products control and traceability (finished products controls)
- Laboratory controls
- Records and reports

LAYOUT:

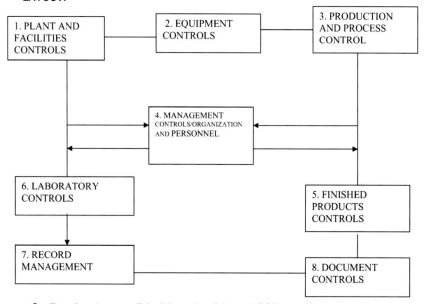

Quality subsystems are linked through policies and SOPs.

PHARMACEUTICAL QUALITY SYSTEM

According to the pharmaceutical quality system draft guidance Q10, the pharmaceutical quality system should comprises the following subsystems:
1. Process performance (process controls)
2. Product quality monitoring (quality indicators)
3. Corrective and preventive action (CAPA)
4. Change control (change and risk assessment)
5. Management review (management controls)

DIAGRAM

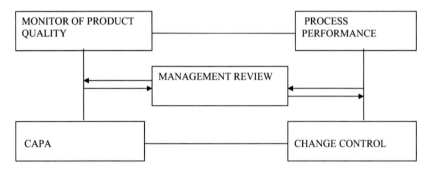

- Adopted from the FDA's draft guidance Q10, pharmaceutical quality system, dated May 9, 2007.

According to this guidance, a pharmaceutical quality system should have at a minimum four quality subsystems, held together by an element of management controls. Management review is a big element out of any management controls. It carries the same weight in pharmaceutical quality subsystems. Management review records are a must for FDA auditors. It is imperative that management review records are kept up to date for any audit. An FDA auditor is interested in finding out ***why an action was taken, who took the action,*** **the results of that action,** and **the date the action was taken.** In other words there has to be traceability for all actions taken to resolve Quality issue

CHAPTER TWO
FUNCTIONS OF QUALITY SUBSYSTEMS

Each quality subsystem has a specified purpose or mission. Quality subsystems comprise processes, which accomplish tasks that produce predetermined outputs. Here are a few functions of chosen quality subsystems:

1. Management controls

The purpose of the management controls subsystem is:
- To provide resources needed to manufacture and distribute products
- To ensure the health of the quality system by reviewing quality indices
- To establish and maintain a quality policy
- To establish and maintain standard operating procedures
- To appoint a management representative to oversee the quality system
- To have an established management review process
- To establish and maintain an internal audit system for feedback on the quality management system

2. Design controls

The purpose of this quality subsystem is:
- To ensure that the final product meets the intended uses
- To ensure that requirements are met
- To establish and maintain design control procedures
- To establish and maintain procedures for design transfer from research and development to commercialization

- To establish process and product validation and verification procedures
- To develop and maintain design review processes
- To maintain records of all design activities
- To maintain records design changes during the design cycle
- To establish and maintain procedures for design validation
- To review and approve design changes during the product life cycle

3. Production and process controls

The purpose of the production and process control quality subsystem is:
- To manufacture products that meet specifications
- To establish and maintain validated processes
- To control and monitor manufacturing processes through statistical process controls or any other chosen means
- To establish and maintain procedures for in-process and final acceptance activities
- To control the five sources of variation: man, method, machine, material, and Mother Nature
- Use of statistical techniques to monitor process parameters
- Process validation
- Established standard operating procedures
- Control of process and product changes

4. Corrective action/preventive action, CAPA

The purpose of the CAPA quality subsystem is:
- To collect and analyze information on the health of the quality system
- To identify and investigate the actual and potential product and quality problems
- To take effective action to prevent occurrence of potential quality problems and stop recurrence of an existing problem
- To have maintained methods for data analysis
- To establish and maintain standard operating procedures for root-cause analysis
- To communicate quality information to management for management review
- To validate and verify all actions taken in corrective or preventive action
- To communicate information about quality to parties

concerned
- To receive, review, and evaluate customer complaint files
- To maintain records of all actions taken to resolve a problem, potential problem, or customer complaint

5. Document controls

The purpose of this quality subsystem is
- To develop and maintain procedures through which documents are initiated, evaluated, approved, and distributed
- To ensure that only current documents are used
- To assure that written procedures are current and adequate
- To ensure that only approved documents are in circulation
- To ensure revision control

6. Records controls

This quality subsystem ensures that
- An adequate record-retention policy is implemented and followed
- Documents are maintained over the required period of time
- Quality system records are maintained
- In the case of medical device organizations, design history files, design master records, and design history records are maintained and retained for the time period specified in the record retention period
- Distribution records are maintained and available upon request
- Records stored in automated data processing systems are backed up

7. Change Control

This quality subsystem achieves the following
- It manages risks associated with changes related to product, process, and the quality system
- It assures that changes are reviewed, approved, and incorporated into documents
- It limits variation in process and products and ensures that things are done the same way all the time
- It is a capacity management tool

8. Material controls

This quality subsystem accomplishes the following
- Supplier evaluation and qualification
- Supplier certification
- Evaluation of contractors and consultants
- In-coming material inspection
- Final inspection
- Discrepant material segregation, evaluation, and disposition (MRB system)
- Product traceability and identification during production
- Product traceability and identification after distribution
- Product storage
- Distribution procedures
- Product acceptance status
- Material-handling procedures
- Labeling process and procedures
- Label control and integrity
- Control of nonconforming products
- In-process acceptance activities
- Material receiving acceptance activities
- Nonconforming products review and disposition

9. Equipment controls

This quality subsystem comprises the following
- Equipment installation and qualification
- Equipment maintenance schedules
- Equipment contamination control
- Equipment calibration cycles
- Equipment identification system
- Servicing
- Control of inspection, measuring, and test equipment

10. Facilities controls

This quality subsystem comprises the following
- Building design and site validation
- Environmental controls
- Floor layout and process flow
- Support subsystems (HVAC, RO, DI water, electricity, and discharge permits)

CHAPTER THREE: QUALITY SYSTEM REGULATIONS (QSR)

1. Medical device

Quality system regulations for medical device organizations are specified in Subpart B of title 21 in part 820 of the Code of Federal Regulations (21CFR part 820). Part 820.20 calls for the establishment of a quality system with the following general requirements under management responsibilities:

(a) A defined quality policy

(b) A defined organizational structure

(c) Defined responsibilities and authority

(d) Adequate resources

(e) A designated management representative with authority over performance of the quality system

(f) A formal management review process of the quality system

(g) A formal quality plan

(h) A defined documentation structure

(i) Standard operating procedures

(j) An internal quality audit system

(k) A personnel training system

(l) Training records

Quality subsystems are specified in the following subparts:

Subpart C: Design controls
Subpart D: Document controls
Subpart E: Purchasing controls (material controls)
Subpart F: Identification and traceability (material controls)
Subpart G: Production and process controls
Subpart H: Acceptance activities (material controls)
Subpart I: Nonconforming products (material controls)
Subpart J: Corrective and preventive action (CAPA)
Subpart K: Labeling and packaging controls (material controls)
Subpart L: Handling, storage, distribution, and installation (material controls)
Subpart M: Records (records controls)
Subpart N: Servicing (equipment control/CAPA)

It must be noted that these are minimum quality subsystems required within your quality system. As we saw earlier, the seven quality subsystems can be organized into ten quality subsystems, each with its policy, standard operating procedures, work instructions, and records.

2.0 The manufacture, processing, packaging, and holding of drugs and pharmaceuticals

Quality system requirements for drugs and pharmaceuticals are not as explicit as those of the medical device industry. However, part 211 of the cGMP touches on the following subparts, which are by all intents and purposes quality subsystems:

Subpart B: Organization and personnel

This section is the equivalent of management controls in a medical device quality management system. It is responsible for:

- Organizational structure
- The quality system
- Defined roles and responsibilities
- Personnel training

- External resources, including consultants and contractor hire

Subpart C: Facilities and buildings
This subsection is the equivalent of the facilities controls quality subsystem in the medical device model. It is responsible for the following processes:
- Utilities (water, electricity, etc.)
- Building design and validation
- Maintenance
- Sewage and other waste
- The plumbing system and discharge permits
- Ventilation and sanitation

Subpart D: Equipment
This section is the equivalent of the equipment controls quality subsystem in medical device. Here are its functions:
- Equipment preventive maintenance schedules
- Equipment design, installation, and qualification
- Corrective maintenance schedules
- Automated equipment installation and validation

Subpart E: Control of components and drug-product containers and closures
This is one of the subsections that would fit under material controls in the QSR. Here are the functions under this subsection:
- Incoming receiving
- Incoming material tests
- Control of rejected incoming material
- In-process tests
- Control of drug-product containers

Subpart F: Production and process control
Here are specified functions for this subsystem
- Established standard operating procedures
- Deviation control
- Yield analysis
- Equipment traceability and identification
- In-process sampling and testing
- Contamination control
- Rework methods

Subpart G: Packaging and labeling controls
This is another subsection that would fit under material controls and traceability

Its functions are:
- Label inventory control
- Packaging procedures
- Labeling procedures
- Label usage criteria
- Packaging validation

Subpart H: Holding and distribution
This subsection would still fit under material controls. Its functions are specified as:
- Product storage procedures
- Product distribution procedures

Subpart I: Laboratory controls
This subsection fits under material controls or production and process control. The subsection accomplishes the following:
- Stability tests
- Establishes test requirements
- Establishes contamination procedures
- Establishes in-process test
- Establishes criteria for product release and distribution

Subpart J: Records and reports
This subsection accomplishes the following:
- Implement the organizations record-retention policy
- Maintain all quality records
- Maintain batch records
- Maintain laboratory records
- Maintain distribution records
- Maintain customer complaint files
- Maintain the master production log

Subpart K: Returned and salvaged drug products
This subsection fits under material controls. It stipulated functions are:
- Control of customer returns
- Rework procedures

Since blood is classified as a drug, subsections in part 211 would "pertain to biological products for human use specified in parts 600 through 680." In other words, these subsections offer the basis for quality subsystems for blood banks and transfusion services.

3.0 Human cell, tissues, and cellular and tissue-based products

Requirements for the establishment and maintenance of a quality system are established in section 1271.160 of the cGTP. General requirements for the quality system are outlined as:
- The establishment of procedures
- Maintenance of standard operating procedures
- The initiation, review, approval, and revision of procedures
- Records management
- Procedures for receiving, investigating, evaluating, and documenting shared information
- Investigation of audit findings through the corrective action system
- Documentations of corrective actions taken
- Training and education of personnel
- Established monitoring system
- Record management system
- Discrepant product investigation
- Product deviation evaluation
- Management with authority over the quality system
- An established audit system
- Validation of computers used in tracking and maintain data

Quality subsystems are implied in the following sections:
Section 1271.170: Organization and personnel (management controls)
Section 1271.180: Procedures (document controls)
Section 1271.190: Facilities controls
Section 1271.195: Environmental control and monitoring (facilities controls)
Section 1271.200: Equipment (equipment controls)
Section 1271.220: Process controls
Section 1271.225: Process changes (change control)
Section 1271.230: Process validations (part of process control)
Section 1271.250: Labeling controls
Section 1271.260: Storage (material control)
Section 1271.265: Receipt and distribution
Section 1271.270: Records (record management)
Section 1271.290: Tracking

Section 1271.320: Complaint file (CAPA, customer complaint system)

GENERAL SYSTEM LAYOUT:

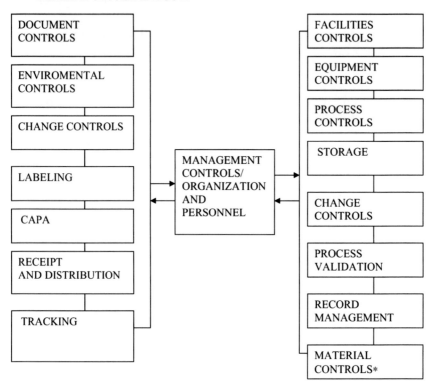

*Not specified but recommended.

CHAPTER FOUR
DOCUMENT HIERARCHY

Document structure is probably the most overlooked and misunderstood part in most quality management systems. Most organizations confuse standard operating procedures with work instructions. There are essentially five document layers in a quality management system. The document hierarchy is based on the number of signatures needed to change or approve the document. At the top of the heap are manuals and policies. The second tier comprises standard operating procedures or cross-functional documents. The third layer comprises records or proof that it happened. The fourth layer comprises job aids. In most quality systems the documentation hierarchy is based on the ISO 9001 model:

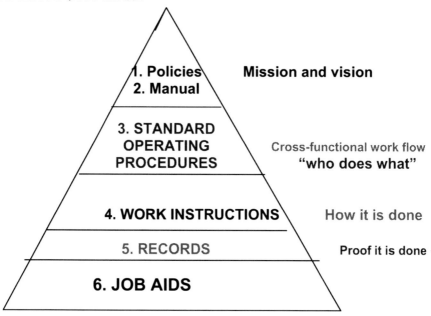

The first set of documents usually includes the quality manual and company policies. These are high-level documents that establish the vision and mission of the organization and the approach the organization has taken to accomplish what it set out to do. The manual gives reasons for the existence of the organization. The policies give the organization's philosophies and beliefs.

1. QUALITY MANUAL

ISO 8402 defines a quality manual as that "document that states the quality policy and describes the quality system of an organization." The quality manual sets the tone for the organization's commitment to quality. It lays out the mission of the organization. For that reason, the quality manual should contain both the mission and the vision of the founders of the organization. It is the highest document in the document structure of any organization. It contains the organization's quality policy statement. An effective quality manual should accomplish the following:

- Communicate the organization's quality policy
- Describe the **quality m**anagement **s**ystem
- Provide **document references**
- Describe the **documentation structure**
- Define **management responsibility**
- Describe governing **quality system regulations and standards**

2. STANDARD OPERATING (SOP)

These are second-tier documents, also called standard operating procedures, or SOPs. Standard operating procedures outline roles and responsibilities for different functional roles and cross-functional units. Standard operating procedures are also called departmental procedures because they address the following:
- **Who** does what?

- **When** is it done?
- **Where** is it done?

Second tier documents are usually written in second-person voice. Examples would be:

"A change request is initiated by manufacturing."

"The change control manager reviews all requested changes."

"The changes are approved by change control board."

3. WORK INSTRUCTIONS (WI)

These are third-tier documents that provide instructions on how to accomplish a particular task in a process. Work instructions address the question, "**How** do I perform this task?" Good work instructions provide step-by-step sequences in which tasks are performed.

An example here would be:

"Push the button labeled START.

Wait for the temperature GAUGE to read 125°F.

Push the button labeled START PROCESS.

After the process monitor reads CYCLE COMPLETE push the PROCESSEND button."

The biggest problem in quality system design is that a half of the time, contents of tier-three documents are mixed with documents of tier two. In other words, documents about **how** something is done are incorporated within documents addressing **who** does **what**, and **when**. The result, as you may imagine, is chaos.

4. RECORDS

Records are essentially the **proof** that a task was performed. They capture the results of any task performed in the quality management system. Here is the information a record should capture:
- What was done (process name)
- Who did it (name)
- When it was done (date, shift)
- What the results were (data)

5. JOB AIDS

Job aids are used to collect information, or provide information at a glance. The most-used job aids are check sheets, reference materials like AQL inspection tables, and process maps. Check sheets are usually used as a guide to record accomplishments of specified process steps or tasks. Process check sheets should have the following information:
- What information is collected
- When the information is collected
- By whom it is collected
- Where it is collected
- Values of data collected
- Units of measure

Job aids vary from process to process and from task to task.

CHAPTER FIVE: CONTENTS OF A QUALITY MANUAL

Regardless of the quality management system your organization follows, the quality manual should be the highest document in the document hierarchy of your quality management system, or QMS. Quality manuals lay out components of your quality program, including management responsibility. The first page of your quality manual should be the contents page. The following are sections of a quality manual that should appear on your contents page:

CONTENTS
- 1.0 Introduction
- 2.0 Control of quality manual
- 3.0 References
- 4.0 Definitions
- 5.0 Quality systems requirements
- 6.0 Management responsibility
- 7.0 Design controls
- 8.0 Document and records controls
- 9.0 Purchasing and materials controls
- 10.0 Identification and traceability
- 11.0 Production and process controls
- 12.0 Inspection, measuring, and test equipment controls
- 13.0 Acceptance activities
- 14.0 Labeling and packaging controls
- 15.0 Corrective and preventive action (CAPA)
- 16.0 Storage, handling, and distribution

1.0 Introduction

In this section you should lay out your mission statement, the products your organization produces, and the quality management requirements used as reference for your quality system. An example here would be:

> 1.1 "Avante Medical Products Incorporated designs, manufactures, and markets surgical equipment. Avante Medical Products' headquarters is located in San Jose, California.
> Our products include surgical retractors, catheters, clumps, and other specialty catalogue products. We sell our products to private surgeons and health-care providers in the United States, Canada, Australia, Japan, and South America.
> 1.2 Avante Medical Products' quality management system is designed to meet the following quality standards and requirements,
>   1.2.1 ISO13485: 2003
>   1.2.2 ISO 9001
>   1.2.2 21 CFR parts 820(QSR regulations)
>   1.2.3 The Canadian Medical Device Regulations
>   1.2.4 93/42/EEC

Pharmaceutical organizations may quote 21CFR part 211 and 21 CFR parts 210 and other standards in this section. Biomedical companies may use 21 CFR parts 660 as a reference point. Tissue and cellular therapy organizations may use parts of 21 CFR part 1271 as their reference point for requirements for the quality system

2.0 Control of quality manual

In this section specify the number of quality manuals available and where they are located. An example here would be:

> "There are five copies of the quality manual located in the following offices:
>   2.1 Office of the company president
>   2.2 Office of the vice president of quality

2.3 Office of the chief operations officer
2.4 Office of regulatory affairs
2.5 Office of the quality manager

Any other information relevant to the organization and deemed necessary may be added to this section as deemed warranted.

3.0 References

This section requires a summary in table format of regulatory requirements and other quality standards on which the your quality system is based. An example for medical device organizations is given below:

Item	Standard/Regulation
1. Quality system requirements	21CFR part 820
2. Labeling	21 CFR part 801
3. Quality Management system	ISO 13485 and ISO 9001
4. Medical device directive	Council Directive 93/42/EEC
5. Medical device regulations	Canadian Medical Device Regulations

The list of requirements in your requirement table should be unique to standards and quality system requirements for your industry.

4.0 Definitions

This section is reserved for a table with all the terms used to define elements of your quality management system. An example for medical device organizations is given below:

Use terms and acronyms that are unique to your quality system

Terms or Acronym	Definition
Quality manual	A company's high-level document that lays out the overall mission and quality system model
Product realization	Stages (planning, design, reviews, etc.) through which the product is designed and transferred to manufacturing
Design qualification	Review process to reconcile design requirements and end-user requirements
Design review	Systematic review to see if design inputs met design outputs
Management review	A formal review of all quality system data by the management team
Management responsibility	The overall roles and responsibilities for the management team
Process	A set of steps that add value to an input to produce an output
CAPA	Corrective Action/Preventive Action

Validation	Verification by objective evidence that the process/product **consistently** met predetermine requirements
Verification	Determining whether requirements were set
Quality indicators	Matrices/dashboards used to measure the health of the quality system
Quality plan	The approach taken in building quality into a product or service
Management representative	AKA management with executive authority over the quality system
Environmental controls	Inputs into manufacturing environment, e.g., pressure, particle count, or humidity, that are controlled to bring about the desired results

5.0   Quality system requirements

In this section define your quality system and its quality subsystems in relation to regulatory and your business requirements. An example is given below:

    5.1 The quality management system comprises ten quality subsystems that are made up of interrelated processes that work together as a unit to accomplish predetermined quality outcomes

    5.2 The quality management system comprises the following

quality subsystems
5.2.1   Management controls
5.2.2   Design controls
5.2.3   Material controls
5.2.4   Production and process controls
5.2.5   Equipment controls
5.2.6   Facilities controls
5.2.7   Corrective Action/Preventive Action (CAPA)
5.2.8   Change controls
5.2.9   Document control
5.2.10 Record management

5.3 Quality system layout (GENERAL)

Here provide a diagrammatic representation of all quality subsystems in your quality system. An example is given below:

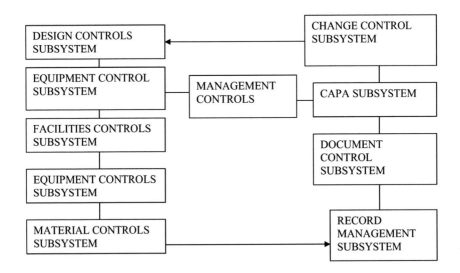

The QSIT (quality system inspection technique) **specifies six quality subsystems**. These should be the baseline for your quality subsystem they are:
- Design controls
- CAPA
- Material controls
- Production and process controls
- Equipment and facilities controls

- Records, documents, and change control
- Management controls

These quality subsystems make the baseline. The number of quality subsystems you choose should be based on the quality management system your organization chooses to adopt. However, it is recommended that your quality system be subdivided into quality subsystems that are functional and unique to the culture and structure of your organization. The design of a quality management system should not be purely a document-generation exercise. It should be about creating cross-functional units that work together as one to produce products and services that meet the needs of the external customer.

5.4 Document hierarchy

Here provide the documentation structure of your quality management system. An example is given below:

The quality system document system is made up of five tiers of controlled documents:

Diagrammatic representation:

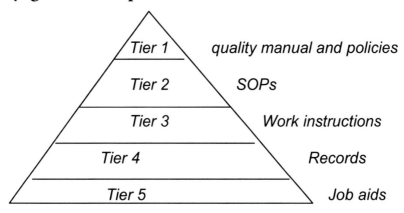

5.4.1 Tier-one documents
This tier comprises the organization's quality manual, all policies

5.4.2 Tier-two documents
This tier comprises cross-functional documents that address workflow between departments and functional roles

5.4.3 Tier-three documents
These group of documents is made up of all work instructions. They provide instructions as to "how" the job should be done

5.4.4 Tier-four documents
This group of documents provides proof that the task or work was performed

5.4.5 Tier-five documents
These are forms and any other templates required to perform a particular task.

5.5 Document traceability map

Here provide a table with the organization's documents, document numbers, ownership of the quality subsystems, and processes where they are used. An example is given on the next page:

The format you use for your table should be unique to your organization. However, a document traceability map you put in your quality manual should have at a minimum the following pieces of information:
- The quality subsystem
- The policy governing that subsystem
- The processes in the subsystem that are affected by the policy
- Standard operating procedures per quality subsystem
- Process affected by the standard operating procedures
- Documented work instructions for each process in a subsystem
- Document numbers and revisions levels
- Records per process

SUBSYSTEM	PROCESS	POLICY	STANDARD OPERATING PROCEDURE	WORK INSTRUCTION	RECORDS	DOC. NUMBER
Management Controls	All	1. Quality policy 2. Quality manual	SOP 546	WI 0045	1. Training record 2. Ownership record	QM002 QM001
		3. Training policy 4. Audit policy	SOP 678	WI 0093	3. Training records 4. Audit record	TP006 QR009
Change control	1. Stakeholder analysis 2. Change approval	5. Change control policy	SOP 324 Change control	WI 896	1. CCB minutes log 2. Agenda	CCR 453 CCB 456
CAPA	1. CAPA 2. Root-cause analysis	6. CAPA policy	SOP 643	WI 567		FRM 9804
Design control	1. Design review 2. Design transfer	7. Design control policy	SOP 952	WI 7766	DHF	QM11X
Document control	1. Document initiation 2. Document review 3. Document approval	8. Document control policy	SOP 345	WI 294 WI556 WI 337	Approval record	DD776
Management	1. Management review 2. Annual review	9. Management Review policy	SOP975	WI 765 WI 876	Annual review record	MR007
CAPA	Customer complaint process	10. Customer complaint policy	SOP 656	WI 888	Complaint record	CCR0098

5.6 ISO 13485 requirements/ISO 9000 requirements

Though ISO 9001 is a voluntary quality management system, it is comprehensive and recommended for most organizations. *Here all the requirements used as reference for your quality management system should be cited in a tabular form. An example is given below:*

REQUIREMNT	STANDARD	DOCUMENT
4.2.2 (a), (b), (c)	ISO13485	Quality manual
4.1(a), (b), (c), (e), (f)	ISO13485	Standard operating procedures and process maps
4.2.3 Document control	ISO 13485	Approval process, revision management process, absolution policy
4.2.4 Record management	ISO 13485	Record management policy
5.0 Management controls	ISO 13485	Communication, quality policy, management review process, resource allocation

Next to the requirements, show the relationship between the requirements and your quality management system. An example for medical device organizations is given below:

David N. Muchemu

ISO 13485 QUALITY SYSTEM MODEL

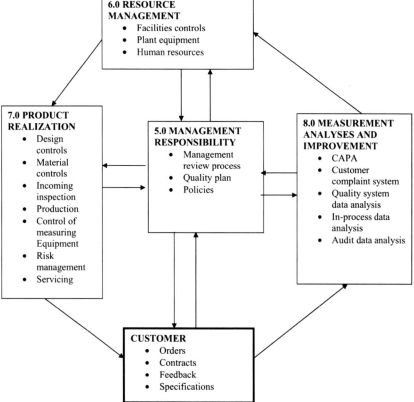

The ISO 13485 quality system is customer focused. Unlike the previous ISO family of standards, ISO 13485 treats the external customer as an integral part of the organization's quality management system. *Here link your processes to the external feedback loop.*

6.0 Management Responsibility

6.1 Management commitment

Here insert a commitment statement signed by your company leader. The statement could be a letter signed by the chief executive officer (CEO) or chairman of the board.

6.2 Organization.

Here insert your organizational chart including the several functions in the quality unit. An example is given below:

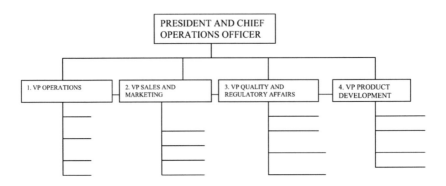

Most senior managers prefer what is called a flat organizational structure. A flat organizational structure has been defined as "hands-on management." It eliminates bureaucratic red tape in organizations that stifle product and process flow. For that reason it is recommended for most organizations. The structure you choose for your organization should be dependent on the culture of the organization you strive to build and grow. In the above diagram all direct reports to the cross-functional vice presidents have access to the subsystem head; they do not communicate through another bureaucratic layer.

6.3 Quality policy

Here insert your quality policy. A quality policy defines the quality approach the organization takes. It should be short and to the point.

Example: *Our commitment is to improve the quality of patient care around the world through robust designs, customer involvement, and continuous process improvement.*

6.4 Management Review

Here state:
    6.4.1   *The composition of your management review team*
    6.4.2   *Management review objectives*

6.4.3 Frequency of management review meetings
6.4.4 Ownership of the quality review meetings
6.4.5 Management review input (CAPA, change control, NCR, and audits)

6.5 Quality planning
6.5.1 Insert elements of your quality plan here. The quality plan could include key processes, process parameter, and control points.
6.5.2 State quality objectives
6.5.3 State methods used to evaluate the quality management system
6.5.4 State the authority of management with executive Responsibility
6.5.5 Identify management representative

6.6 Quality audits
Here describe your quality audit process, frequency, and ownership. Your description should include internal and third-party audits. It should also address how audit findings are addressed.

6.7 Personnel
Here describe the training system in the organization. Your description should touch on the different layers of your personnel and the curriculum available.

7.0 Design controls

7.1 Design model
Insert the mode of design process. An example is given below

Designing A World-Class Quality Management System

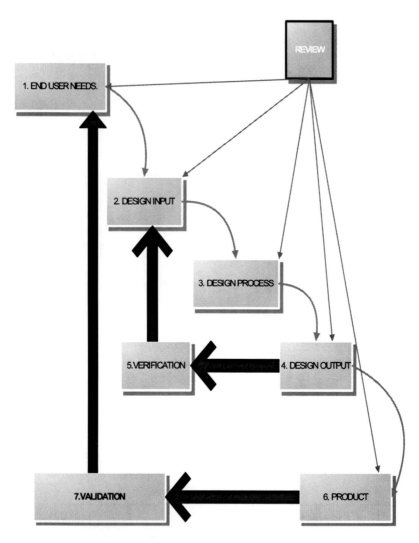

(Based on the Canadian Ministry of Health cascading waterfall design model.)

Describe the **ten** elements that comprise design control in the above model:

7.2 Design development planning

Here describe all design development phases, tasks, ownership, and cross-functional workflow. Your description should also mention quality records kept in each phase

7.3 Design input

Here describe how the needs of the end user/customer are reviewed and translated into design requirements. Your description should also include the peer-review process and records kept, including laboratory notebooks.

7.4 Design output

In this subsection, describe your process for evaluating conformance of final product design output/performance to design requirements established during the previous phase. Your description should include design verification methods used.

7.5 Design Review

Describe your design review process, with emphasis on the following elements:

7.5.1 Review process map
7.5.2 Review team composition
7.5.3 Review activities
7.5.4 Review records
7.5.5 Design history file

7.6 Design Verification

Here describe elements of design verification, including the records kept. List procedures that reconcile design inputs and design outputs, including design history file records from the activities undertaken in the phase.

7.7 Design Change control

Describe the linkage between design changes and the organization's formal change control, including the following elements:

7.7.1 Major changes to an approved application
7.7.2 Criteria for 510(k) submission
7.7.3 Minor changes to the design
7.7.4 Change review process

7.8 Design Validation

Describe the established procedure and work flow for validating the product. Include the following elements in your description:

    7.8.1 Validation plan
    7.8.2 Validation protocols
    7.8.3 Validation reports
    7.8.4 Linkage between design validation and design history file (DHF)

7.9 Design transfer

    7.9.1 Identification methods (bar codes, etc.)
    7.9.2 Supplier relationships
    7.9.3 Supplier evaluations
    7.9.4 Approved supplier list
    7.9.5 Incoming material inspection
    7.9.6 The MRB process

8.0. Identification and Traceability

Here discuss how your organization handles the following

    8.1 Material tracking (incoming)
    8.2 Finished products traceability
    8.3 In-process product traceability
    8.4 Nonconforming material segregation
    8.5 Nonconforming material disposition

Here describe design phase linkages between product development or research and development and manufacturing with emphasis on:

    8.5.1 Design transfer activities
    8.5.2 Roles and responsibilities (quality, manufacturing, product development, etc.).
    8.5.3 Traceability
    8.5.4 Supplier qualification
    8.5.5 Design transfer record

9.0 Design History File

Here define the design history file with emphasis on:
    9.1 Contents of the DHF
    9.2 Ownership of the DHF
    9.3 Design plan
    9.4 Control of changes to the design history file

10.0 Document and records controls

In this section define the following elements:
    10.1 Document initiation process
    10.2 Document approval process
    10.3 Document change control process
    10.4 Document release and distribution process
    10.5 Quality records
    10.6 Record-retention policy
    10.7 Document numbering system
    10.8 Control number system
    10.9 Laboratory notebook controls
    10.10 Document status identification
    10.11 Quality system software controls
    10.12 Electronic records and signatures controls (part 11)

11.0 Purchasing/material controls

Discuss how your organization handles the following:
    11.1 Product Identification system
    11.2 Identification status of incoming materials and product

12.0 Production and process controls

Discuss the elements of production and process controls with emphasis that apply to your organization:
    12.1 Process validation criteria
    12.2 Test-method validation
    12.3 Equipment controls (maintenance schedule, calibration,

qualification, inspection, etc.)
12.4 Manufacturing process
12.5 Quality plan
12.6 Documented process work instructions and operating procedures
12.7 Environmental controls (clean room management, etc.)
12.8 Personnel training and certification
12.9 Manufacturing material controls
12.10 Manufacturing change control
12.11 Approval of processes and process equipment
12.12 Controls for key processes
12.13 Contamination control
12.14 Key automated processes
12.15 Computer systems and software validation
12.16 Revalidation criteria
12.17 Facility designs and support systems
12.18 Manual processes
12.19 Control of nonconforming products
12.20 Nonconformity review and disposition
12.21 Investigation of nonconformities

13.0 Inspection, measuring, and test-equipment controls

Here discuss the following elements:
13.1 Control of calibration equipment
13.2 Control of the accuracy of measuring equipment
13.3 Your calibration process
13.4 Inspection plans
13.5 Control of the accuracy of the test equipment
13.6 Calibration standards used
13.7 Calibration records

14.0 Acceptance activities

Discuss how your organization handles the following items:
14.1 In-process inspection
14.2 Final inspection

14.3 Acceptance records
14.4 Supplier corrective action system (SCAR)
14.5 Supplier certification
14.6 Supplier agreements
14.7 Supplier change control
14.8 Control of nonconforming material, segregation, and disposition
14.9 Incoming inspection procedures
14.10 Control, segregation, and disposition of nonconforming materials and components

15.0 Labeling and Packaging control

In this section discuss the following items
15.1 Labeling system/operation
15.2 Labeling inspection
15.3 Labeling change control
15.4 Labeling storage
15.5 Labeling controls
15.6 Labeling standard operating procedure and work instructions
15.7 Packaging
15.8 Packaging inserts
15.9 Packaging validation
15.20 Sterilization system
15.21 Storage-control system
15.22 Distribution records

16.0 Corrective Action and Preventive Action (CAPA)

Here you should discuss your CAPA system with emphasis on:
16.1 Corrective action and preventive action standard operating procedures
16.2 Process analysis standard operating procedures
16.3 Root-cause analysis methodology
16.4 Linkage between CAPA and change control
16.5 Linkage between CAPA and customer-complaint system

16.6 CAPA discovery vehicles (how issues are discovered)
16.7 CAPA records
16.8 Information system
16.9 Linkage between CAPA and audit system
16.10 Linkage between CAPA and field actions

17.0 Handling, storage, and distribution

Here you should discuss the following:
17.1 Standard operating procedures used to prevent product mix-up, deterioration, and contamination
17.2 Procedures for the stockroom inventory control
17.3 Procedures for receipt and distribution of finished products
17.4 Distribution record management

18.0 Internal communication

Here describe communication system used between employees and management, including:
18.1 The e-mail system
18.2 Teleconferencing
18.3 Newsletters
18.4 Intranet
18.5 Memos

CHAPTER SIX
QUALITY SUB-SYSTEM POLICIES

Quality subsystem policies are different from the quality policy in two ways. First, they establish order and ownership. Second, unlike the quality policy, which is usually brief and to the point, quality subsystem policies can be extensive. Quality subsystem policies are usually the tier-one documents in quality subsystems that establish the mission of the quality subsystem:

THE SEVEN QUALITY SUBSYSTEMS:

(A) The QSR quality system model for medical devices has seven subsystems with four satellite subsystems:

Reproduced (with permission) from the Quality System Inspection Technique (QSIT) at www. FDA.gov

Designing A World-Class Quality Management System

The seven QSIT quality subsystems include:

1. Management (management responsibility)

This is also known as management controls. The following key processes under this quality subsystem require a policy:
- Quality planning
- Personnel training
- Document and records retention
- Internal audits

The Seven Subsystems: General Model for all industries

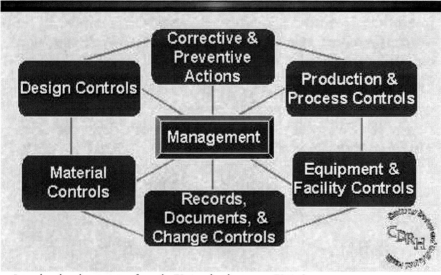

Reproduced with permission from the FDA web side at www.FDA.Gov

(B) With management controls as the center of the quality management system

Source: FDA.gov

2. Equipment and facilities controls

The following key processes may require a guiding policy:
- Control of inspection, measuring, and test equipment
- Preventive maintenance

3. Records, document, and change controls

The following policies are recommended for this quality subsystem:
- Record-retention policy
- Change control policy

4. Material controls

The following policies are recommended for this quality subsystem:
- Supplier quality management policy
- Supplier corrective action policy
- Supplier audits policy
- Supplier change control policy

5. Design controls

The following policies are required for this quality subsystem:
- Policy on design change control
- Policy on design reviews

6. Corrective action and preventive action (CAPA)

The following is recommended for this quality subsystem:
- CAPA policy
- Policy on medical device reporting (medical device organizations)
- Policy on corrections and removals (medical device organizations)

7. Production and process controls

The following policies are recommended for this quality subsystem:
- Policy on process validation
- Change control policy
- Production equipment controls policy

The number of quality subsystem policies for your organization should be determined by the complexity and criticality of your key processes. Above all, the primary purpose of a quality subsystem policy should be taken into account when deciding whether or not to have a policy for a key process. The purpose of any is threefold:
- Paints a clear high-level picture of what needs to be done (provides vision)
- Establishes boundaries for tasks to be performed (provides a

scope)
- Establishes ownership (responsibility)

The following are examples of quality subsystem policies:

Example 1: Change control policy

1.0 POLICY STATEMENT

Example: "It is the policy of Amana, Inc. to manage risks and variation related to changes in processes and products to a predictable level through a world-class change control quality subsystem."

2.0 SCOPE

This section establishes boundaries for the quality system subsections involved.

Example: "This policy applies to change requests from the following quality subsystems":

    2.1 Product development
    2.2 CAPA system
    2.3 Production and process control /manufacturing
    2.4 Document control
    2.5 Product and process validation
    2.6 Supplier management
    2.7 Facilities and equipment controls

3.0 RESPONSIBILITY

This section establishes ownership.

Example: "The vice president of product quality or designee is responsible for enforcing this policy."

4.0 DEFINITIONS

This section establishes the vocabulary to be used in the standard operating procedure (SOP—second-layer document) and associated work instructions (third-layer documents).

EXAMPLE:

The following words and acronyms are used in enforcing this policy:

Word, Phrase, or Acronym	Definition
1.Change control	A system through which the effects or risks of changes initiated in an organization are controlled to a predictable level
2.Change order	A document issued to implement an approved change request
3.Stakeholders	All the people or organizations with a vested interest in the proposed change
4.ECO	A change order usually associated with product specifications
5.Change board	A cross-functional team that evaluates all proposed changes
6.CCB	Change control board

5.0 OVERVIEW

This section gives a high-level view of the tasks covered by the policy

Example:

    5.1 Moderate changes are processed through the change control board

    5.2 Major changes are controlled through the change control board

    5.3 Minor change may only require two signatures for approval, one of which must be the manager of the department in which the change request originates.

    5.4 Minor changes require at a minimum signatures from the department head and quality

    5.5 The change board meets twice a week

    5.6 A change request can be rejected, deferred, accepted, or amended and approved

5.7 The initiator is responsible for addressing issues in the amended change

5.8 Once it is approved, the initiator and the owner or sponsor of the change has thirty days to implement the change

5.9 Deferred changes and rejected changes can be appealed with supporting data

6.0 REFERENCES

This section establishes the regulatory, ISO, and other quality management requirements that guide your change control system

Example: "The following regulatory requirements are referenced for our change control system":

6.1 21 CFR 820.30(I)
6.2 21 CFR 820.30(J)
6.3 21CFR 820.40(b)
6.4 21CFR 820.70
6.5 21 CFR 820.75

Example 2: Quality policy

Management owns the quality policy. Unlike other policies, quality policies tend to be brief and to the point. The aim is to capture the **vision**, **mission**, and **ownership** in as few words as possible that can be memorized by all employees. An example is given below.

"We make quality products that improve the quality of life around the world."

This quality policy is short and to the point, and above all it captures the THREE essential elements required in a quality policy:

- **Ownership**---------"We"

- **Mission**------------"Improve the quality of life"

- **Vision**---------------"Around the world"

The current trend in regulated industries appears to be to have a quality policy that can fit on a business card and a badge. The idea is to have the policy handy at all times so that if an employee is asked by a regulatory auditor what the quality policy of the organization is, the employee can flip the badge or pull out a business card from the wallet and recite it for the auditor.

Example 3: Process validation policy

1.0 POLICY STATEMENT

Example: It is the policy of Amana, Inc., to validate all process whose outputs cannot be independently verified in order to control variation to predictable levels.

2.0 SCOPE

This section establishes boundaries for the quality system subsections involved.
Example: This policy applies to the following activities:
- 2.1 Introduction of new technologies
- 2.2 Introduction of new test methods
- 2.3 Introduction of new equipment
- 2.4 Changes in products and process specifications
- 2.5 New material qualification
- 2.6 Change in manufacturing cite
- 2.7 Changes in design
- 2.8 Introduction of new products

3.0 RESPONSIBILITY

This section establishes ownership.
Example:
- 3.1 The vice president of product quality or designee is responsible for enforcing this policy
- 3.2 The VP of product development is responsible for making sure that all test methods are validated
- 3.3 Supplier quality is responsible for ensuring validation of

changes affecting fit, form, and function

3.4 Manufacturing engineering is responsible for product and process validations

3.5 Quality is responsible for ensuring the validation cycle is followed

3.6 Product development is responsible for validations stemming from new products, enhancements, and product fixes

4.0 DEFINITIONS

This section establishes the vocabulary to be used in the standard operating procedure (SOP—second-layer document) and associated work instructions (third-layer documents).

EXAMPLE:

The following words and acronyms are used in enforcing this policy:

Word, Phrase, or Acronym	Definition
Validation	Objective evidence that the process consistently operates to produce predetermined outcomes.
Verification	Objective evidence that requirements were met
DQ	Design qualification
IQ	Installation qualification
OQ	Operation qualification
PQ	Performance qualification

5.0 OVERVIEW

This section gives a high-level view of the tasks accomplished by the policy

Example:

5.1 Process validation is the responsibility of quality, manufacturing, and process engineering.
5.2 Validation activities apply to:
   5.2.1   Introduction of new products
   5.2.2   Introduction of new processes
   5.2.3   Introduction of new test methods
   5.2.4   Introduction of new technology
   5.2.5   Packaging
5.3 Process-revalidation applies to all key process in a calendar year
5.4 All process that require validation are specified in the master validation plan
5.5 The process is validated when the results cannot be fully verified by inspection and tests
5.6 All activities performed during validation are documented and approved by the heads of quality, manufacturing, and process engineering
5.7 Validation involves both the process and process controls
5.8 The approval criteria of any validation is a demonstration of process repeatability supported by data from sufficient production runs

6.0 REFERENCES

This section establishes the regulatory, ISO, and other quality management requirements that applies to your validation program

Example: The following regulatory requirements and standards are referenced for our validation program:
   6.1   21 CFR 820.75(a)
   6.2   21 CFR 820.75(b)
   6.3   ISO13485

CHAPTER SEVEN
STANDARD OPERATING PROCEDURES

Standard operating procedures, or SOPs as they are commonly referred to, are cross-functional documents. They are written to specify the workflow between departments or job functions. The key characteristic of all standard operating procedures is that they are written in a **second-person voice**. Writing an SOP involves the following **five** steps:
- Identification of functions involved
- Talking to process owners about their vision
- Drafting a process map for the standard operating procedure
- Reviewing a process map with process owners
- Turning a process map into a procedure

IDENTIFYING FUNCTIONS INVOLVED

Identifying functions involved in a particular process starts with asking the question: "Which function has vested interest in this?" A brainstorm team session on this question is a good tool for discovery of key players and what the players bring to the table. The example below is taken from supplier quality management.

Quality subsystem: Supplier quality management
Question: Who has vested interest in supplier quality?
Answer:
- Purchasing
- Product development
- Change control
- Quality
- Manufacturing

MATRIX

FUNCTION	VESTED INTEREST	PROCESS
1. Purchasing/ supply chain	1. Supplier communications 2. Price 3. On-time delivery 4. Stability	1. Supplier relationships 2. Supplier development
2. Product development	1. Performance 2. Quality 3. Reliability	1. New product development 2. Product transfer 3. New product validation
3. Change control	Supplier quality agreement	Supplier change control
4. Quality	1. Quality agreement 2. Process capability 3. Supplier quality	1. Supplier qualification 2. Supplier certification 3. Supplier corrective action requests (SCAR)
5. Manufacturing	Throughput	Manufacturing

TALKING TO PROCESS OWNERS

The second step is to talk to process owners about the perceived workflow between functions. For best results process owners should be asked open-ended questions. Once information has been collected from all process owners, it should be reconciled and forwarded to process owners for review and any amendments. The accuracy of the information determines the accuracy of the process map.

DRAFTING THE PROCESS MAP

The key component of drafting a process map for a quality subsystem is being able to visualize the sequence of steps as specified by process

David N. Muchemu

owners. The key is to identify processes and process steps. The example below distinguishes the difference between a process step and a process. Processes are made up of process steps and require work instructions to accomplish the specified tasks. A step, on the other hand, can be part of a series in a process flow.

(I) Process Flow:

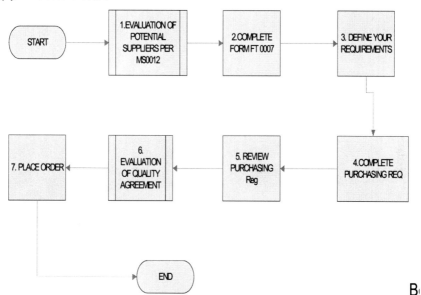

Boxes 1 and 6 represent defined processes with work instructions, whereas boxes 2, 3, 4, 5, and 7 represent steps.

(ii) Process map

The key difference is that in addition to having tangible outputs, processes require work instructions. Process steps on the other hand are written using active verbs and are part of the work instructions.

Unlike a process flow, a process map establishes ownership for tasks in any given quality management subsystem. The example below shows the workflow for a nonconforming material handling subsystem:

Designing A World-Class Quality Management System

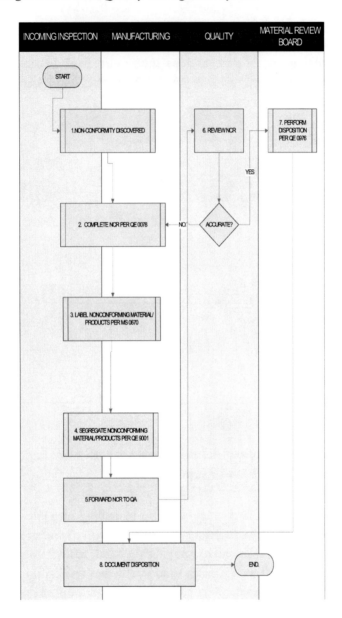

REVIEWING THE PROCESS MAP WITH OWNERS

Once the process map has been developed, it should be reviewed by all process owners. Comments from process owners should be incorporated into the map and the map send back for a second, third, or sometimes even a fourth review. Once the process map is approved it becomes the basis of the standard operating procedure.

TURNING A PROCESS MAP INTO PROCEDURE

Generally speaking, the process map or workflow makes up the procedure section of the standard operating procedure. It assigns ownership to tasks and specifies the sequence of events that take place in a process. Parts of a standard operating procedure are specified below:

SECTIONS OF A STANDARD OPERATING PROCEDURE

A standard operating procedure comprises eight sections, namely:

TITLE: *This is usually at the top of the page. It states what the document accomplishes.* An example here would be: "***Handling of nonconforming materials and products.***"

This statement establishes the intent of the standard operating procedure. In other words, the title proclaims the mission accomplished by the document.

1.0 Purpose

This section gives a detailed description of what the procedure accomplishes. An example here would be: "***This procedure describes the flow of activities associated with discovery of nonconformities related to material, products, and components. It describes the labeling, segregation, and disposition phases.***"

2.0 Scope

This section establishes boundaries around inputs into a particular process or quality subsystem. An example here would be: "**This procedure applies to**

2.1 Nonconformities discovered during work in progress (WIP)

2.2 Nonconformities discovered during incoming inspection

2.3 Customer returns"

3.0 References

This section specifies internal documents and external documents upon which your standard operating procedure is based. An example here would be:

3.1 Internal
    3.1.1 MS 0670 Nonconforming material labeling procedure
    3.1.2 QE 0078 NCR completion work instruction
    3.1.3 QE 9001 Material segregation procedure
    3.1.4 QE 0976 Material disposition procedure

3.2 External
    3.2.1   21CFR 820.50 Purchasing controls
    3.2.2   21CFR820.80 Receiving, in-process, and finished device acceptance
    3.2.3   21CFR 820.80(b) Receiving acceptance activities

4.0 Definitions

Here insert a table that contains terms and acronyms used in the standard operating procedure. An example is given below:

Terms and Acronyms	Definition
SCAR	Supplier corrective action request
Nonconformity	Not meeting requirements
NCR	Nonconformity report
MRB	Material review board

5.0 Responsibility

This section establishes boundaries. An example here would be:

5.1 It is the responsibility of the department where the nonconformity is discovered to label and segregate nonconforming material

5.2 Quality is responsible for reviewing all nonconforming material reports

5.3 The material review board is responsible for disposition

5.4 Quality is responsible for scheduling MRB meetings

6.0 Procedure

This section provides the workflow in second-person voice. It is the process map in words. An example from the above process would be:

6.1 Nonconformities are discovered during in-process inspection on the manufacturing floor or during incoming inspection.

6.2 Upon discovery a nonconformity report is completed by the operator

6.3 The nonconforming product, component, or material is labeled by the operator

6.4 The material is segregated in designated areas to avoid unintended mix-up

6.5 The nonconformity report is forwarded to quality for review and documentation

6.6 Quality holds scheduled MRB meetings for disposition

6.7 After disposition, manufacturing or incoming inspection and quality update the NCR records to reflect final material disposition

7.0 Attachments

Here provide copies of forms and process map. An example of a form that should be included here would be the NCR form.

8.0 Document number and revision level

The document number is usually at the top of the document together with the title. It is also usually at the bottom of every page, along with page numbers and revision level. Some organizations prefer insertion of a table containing traceability information on the last page. An example is provided below:

Rev	Description	ECO #	Originator	Date
A	First release	CO876	David N. Muchemu	01/20/2007
B	Added process map	CO7635	Eddie Mambo Mengi	01/11/2007
C	Corrected typos in procedure section	CO1789	Aisha Mohammed	0/12/2007

CHAPTER EIGHT
WORK INSTRUCTIONS (WIS)

Work instructions are usually written using **active-voice verbs.** There are four steps in writing work Instructions:
- Determine the sequence of flow in your process
- Determine decision points in your process flow
- Review complexity of any loops in your flow
- Audit your flow for sequence
- Review your flow with stakeholders
- Convert the flow into a work instruction using **active-voice verbs**

FLOW CHART SYMBOLS

The following are key symbols used in drafting a process flow:

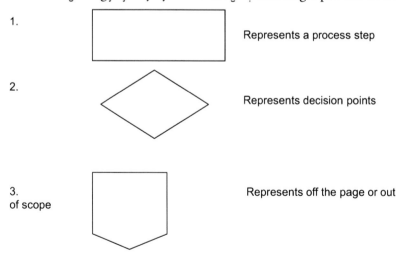

1. Represents a process step
2. Represents decision points
3. of scope Represents off the page or out

An example of a process flow chart is given below:

PURPOSE: Establish a flow chart for the dry-etching process

Designing A World-Class Quality Management System

Diagram:

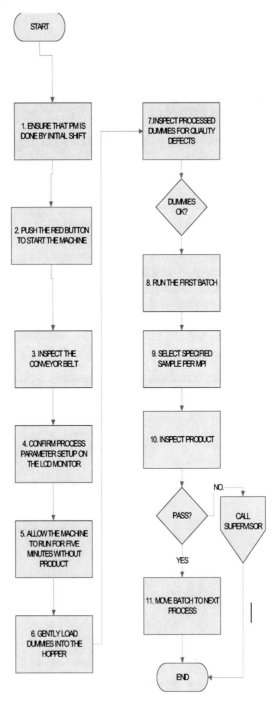

SECTIONS OF A WORK INSTRUCTION

A work instruction document comprises the following sections:
- Title and document number
- Purpose
- Scope
- Responsibilities
- Definitions
- Material/apparatus
- Safety
- Process flow
- Procedure
- Records
- Revision history

TITLE AND DOCUMENT NUMBER

This section appears at the top of the work instruction in the header section. An example is given below:

YOUR COMPANY NAME AND LOGO	DOC.NO: WI -0796
TITLE: *SETUP PROCEDURE FOR THE DRY-ETCHING PROCESS*	Rev. A

1.0 PURPOSE

This is the first section of the body. State the purpose of the work instruction.

Example: *This work instruction provides step-by-step instructions for process set up and completion for dry-etching.*

2.0 SCOPE

This section provides boundaries for the work instruction.

Example: *These work instructions apply to all personnel Qualified to process products on the dry-etcher.*

3.0 RESPONSIBILITY

This section assigns process ownership.

Example: *It is the responsibility of any personnel qualified to process product on the dry-etcher to ensure that this setup procedure is followed without deviation.*

4.0 DEFINITIONS

This section defines words, phrases, and acronyms used in the procedure section of the work instructions.

Example:

Word, Phrase, or Acronym	Definition
1. Dry-Etch	A process that removes excessive metal using a specified gas
2. Operator	Any personnel qualified to use the etcher
3. Process	A set of steps that add value to an input to produce a pre-determined output
4. Process parameters	Pre-determined conditions for optimum process output
5. PPE	Personal protection equipment
6. NCR	Nonconformance report
7. MRB	Material review board
8. ECO	Engineering change order

5.0 MATERIALS/APPARATUS

This specifies materials and tools needed to accomplish the tasks in the process.

Example:

The following materials and tools are required for this work instruction

    5.1 Graduated thermometer

5.2 Volumetric flask
5.3 Latex gloves
5.4 A beaker
5.5 PPE

6.0 SAFETY

This section specifies precautions that need to be taken.

Example: *The following precautions should be taken while operating the dry-etcher*
6.1 Keep your hands from moving parts
6.2 Always use a mask
6.3 When in doubt call your supervisor

7.0 PROCESS FLOW

This section provides a pictorial representation of the sequence of events that take place in the process.
Example:

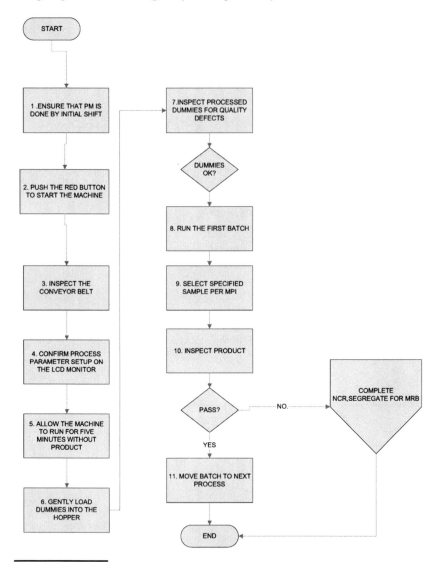

8.0 PROCEDURE

This section translates the process flow in active verbs for action. The example below is based on the process flow above.

Example:

    8.1 Review the preventive maintenance log to ensure that PM was performed on previous shift.

    8.2 If PM was performed, push the RED button to start the machine.

8.3 Inspect the conveyor belt for any damages or irregularities.

8.4 Confirm that process setup parameters on the LCD match the ones posted on machine.

8.5 Allow the machine to warm up by running it for five minutes without product.

8.6 Load process dummies into the hopper.

8.7 Inspect process dummies per criteria on QE 9875.

8.8 If dummies meet the established quality criteria, run the first batch.

8.9 Select specified samples for inspection per MPI.

8.10 Inspect product for specified quality attributes.

8.11 Complete the traveler. Move products that pass to the next process.

8.12 Complete NCR form for products that don't pass. Segregate nonconforming products for MRB disposition.

9.0 RECORD

This section specifies quality records for the process.

Example:

The following documents are proof of work performed and are treated as quality records:

9.1 PM log

9.2 NCR form

9.3 Traveler

9.4 In-process inspection record

Revision	Item	Initiator	ECO #	Date
A	New document initiation	David Muchemu	ECO 1346	6/14/2007
B	Changed sequence in process flow	Aisha Mohammed	ECO 9862	12/12/2007
C	Removed typos in section 9.0	Athuman Mambosasa	ECO 8645	01/27/2008

The revision history section of the work instruction is an important part of the document because it shows its evolution. It should be updated any time a change is made to the document.

CHAPTER NINE
DOCUMENTS AND RECORDS CONTROLS

Document controls

(A) QSR

Requirements for document controls are clearly specified in the QSR, or **Q**uality **S**ystem **R**egulations. Subpart D of 21CFR 820.40 states that each manufacturer is required to:

(a)(i) Have established and maintained procedures for document approval and distribution

(ii) Have a documented approval process (initiation, review, and approval)

(iii) Have a procedure for removal of obsolete documents from point of use

(b) (i) Have a review process for all document changes

(ii) Have a process for communicating document changes to affected personnel in a timely manner

(iii) Maintain a record of all document changes with the following information:
- Description of the change
- The numbers of documents affected
- Approval signatures
- Approval dates
- Implementation date

Paragraphs (a) (i) through paragraph (b) (iii) cover the five phases of a document's life cycle illustrated by the diagram below:

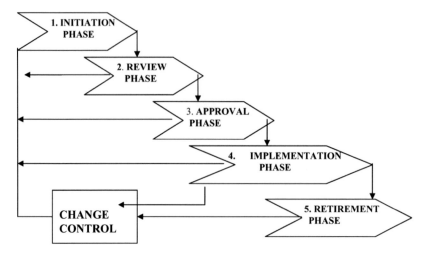

There are tasks associated with every phase of the document life cycle. Those tasks have to be identified, documented, implemented, and controlled to avoid unintended consequences. The tasks chosen by your organization should match the intent of 21CFR 820.40 as the baseline. Some quality personnel in the drug industry, biomedical, and tissue banks have always argued with me that this subsection of the QSR applies to medical device manufacturers ONLY. My argument has always been the same: The QSR is based on the principles of ISO 9001, which is a generic quality management system for any industry under the sun. By default all industries can design a robust quality management system based on 21CFR820.00.

INITIATION PHASE

Tasks performed during this phase may include:
- Issuing of document numbers to initiators for traceability purposes
- Writing and formatting first drafts
- Routing first draft for input and peer review
- Change control

REVIEW PHASE

The review phase is supposed to solicit stakeholder input. For that reason, it is considered the most important phase in the document's life cycle. Tasks performed during this phase may include:
- Routing final draft to stakeholders
- Incorporating stakeholder input into the document
- Final stakeholder review
- Change control

APPROVAL PHASE

This phase may include the following tasks
- Obtaining approval signatures from the quality unit and other signatures
- Issuing of engineering change order (ECO)
- Change control

In some cases, especially in electronic change control systems, the second bullet and the first are accomplished at the same time.

IMPLEMENTATION PHASE

Tasks performed during this phase may include:
- Communicating the release of the new document via the ECO system
- Training of the affected personnel
- Retiring the old version of the document (if it exists)
- Change control

Needless to say, some of these tasks may take place at the same time.

RETIREMENT PHASE

This phase comprises the following tasks:
- Removal of all old versions of the document from points of use to avoid unintended use
- Archiving the old document for traceability purposes
- Change control

The intent of Subpart D of 21CFR 820.40 is to stress the importance of the control of the document life cycle to avoid consequences from unintended use. Your organization has to have mechanisms in place to get this done. Failure to do this improves your chances of becoming a 483 candidate.

(B) Part 1271.180: *Human cells, tissue, and human cell-based products*

This section applies to document control requirements for tissue and cellular products. The section requires that:
- (i) All procedures be reviewed prior to implementation
- (ii) The organization has an established and documented review process
- (iii) Approved documents be made available at the point of use
- (iv) All revisions be documented
- (v) All deviations be authorized and documented
- (vi) Archived procedures be retained for a minimum of ten years

(C) Part 211: Procedures for finished pharmaceuticals and drugs

Part 211.100 calls for the following requirements:
- (I) For the organization to have written procedures for production and process controls
- (II) For changes to any procedure to be drafted, reviewed, and approved
- (III) For any final approval of any changes to any documents to be done by the quality function
- (IV) For any deviations from any approved procedures to be documented and justified.

(D) Part 606.100 Production process control: biologics
Paragraph (b) of this part requires an organization to have:
- (i) Written standard procedures
- (ii) Maintained standard operating procedures
- (iii) Procedures for all processes used in blood collection and processing

The part does not call for specific controls for the documents.

(E) EN ISO 13485:2003 DOCUMENT CONTROL REQUIREMENTS

ISO 13485 is a medical device quality management standard. The requirements for control of documents are found in subsection 4.2.4, which calls for a standard operating procedure that accomplishes the following:

(a) Establishes document review and approval process
(b) Establishes document change control
(c) Establishes revision controls
(d) Establishes a document identification system
(e) Establishes process for document retrieval
(f) Establishes system of control and identification of external documents
(g) Establishes process for controlling obsolete documents

RECORDS CONTROLS: cGMP standard

This is the second piece that comes into play after documents that generate records have been implemented. Proof of work performed by members of the organization has to be protected. The most important piece of records control is documenting, **WHO** did **WHAT, HOW, WHEN**, and a second **WHAT**. The bottom line is there has to be some traceability from task ownership (who), standard task performed, work instructions used, the date (when) the task was performed, and the results (second what) of the task performed.

(i) Medical device records controls

Subpart M section 820.180 calls for the following requirements:
- Maintained records
- Accessible records
- Readily available records
- Electronic backup system for electronic records
- A record-retention policy
- Defined quality records
- Defined criteria for confidential records

Section 820.181 specifies the contents of the device master record as the following:
- Device specifications
- Process specifications
- Quality assurance steps
- Packaging and labeling specifications
- Installation and preventive maintenance procedures

Section 820.184 specifies requirements for contents of the device history record as:
- Date of manufacture
- Quantity manufactured
- Identification

Section 820.186 calls for quality system records. The requirements are specified as:
- A maintained quality system record
- Document matrix

(ii) Drugs and biologics

The following are document-control requirements for drugs and biologics.

Section 211.100 of part 211 requires written procedures for:
- Process control and production

This section also calls for the following:
- The drafting of all changes in procedures
- A review process of changes in procedures
- An approval process of all changes in procedures by stakeholders, including the quality organization
- Adherence to standard operating procedures
- Justification of deviation
- A maintenance record of all deviations

Section 211.142 calls for the establishment of functional warehousing procedures.

Records management

Pharmaceutical requirements for records controls are covered in different sections:

Section 211.180 calls for:
- Retention of batch records for at least one year after expiration

- Maintenance of all drug records for at least a year
- Availability of records for review
- Easy access to records
- Maintenance of all records
- Maintenance of all components

Section 211.182 calls for maintenance of cleaning records of all major equipment

Section 211.186 spells out the quality attributes of a master production record as:
- Batch size
- Date
- Signature
- Secondary signature
- Name of the product
- The strength of the product
- Description of the dosage form
- Method of measure
- Active ingredients per dose
- MPI
- Specifications
- Label copies
- Caution and precautions

Section 211.192 calls for the following record controls:
- Review and approval of records by the quality unit
- Approval of all procedures before batch release
- Written records of all investigations

Section 211.194 calls for the following laboratory records controls:
- Documented lot numbers, including sample source, quantity, traceability information, and dates
- Documented test methods, specifications, and tolerances
- Unit of measure used for each test
- Manipulated data results from each test
- Conclusions drawn from the tests performed
- Signatures of parties performing the tests
- Raw data from all tests
- Records for standards and reference solutions
- Maintained equipment-calibration records
- Records for stability studies performed

Section 211.196 calls for the following distribution records controls:
- The name and strength of the product

- Dosage
- Name of consignee
- Address of consignee
- Quantity shipped
- Control number

CHAPTER TEN
QUALITY SYSTEM LEXICON AND ACRONYMS

The following is a list of common quality systems, terms, phrases, and acronyms. The list is by no means exhaustive. Needless to say, the vocabulary you choose for your quality system should ALWAYS be reflective of your organizations cooperate culture. The terms have been compiled from ISO 9001 (the parent of any quality system), Part 210, part 211, the QSR, and other regulatory material including the FDA website.

A

Word, Phrase, or Acronym	Definition
Advertising and labeling	Any promotional material that may influence the end user.
Assessment	Evaluation process including a document review, an onsite audit, and an analysis and report. Customers may also include a self-assessment, internal audit results, and other materials in the assessment.
Attribute	The property a unit has of being either bad or good. That is, the quality characteristic of a unit is either within the specified requirements or it is not.
compliant	Conformance to set standards.

Attribute data	Data that is countable in whole numbers.
Audit	Systematic and independent examination to determine whether quality activities and related results comply with planned arrangements and whether these arrangements are implemented effectively and are suitable to achieve objectives.
Audit conclusion	*The outcome of an audit provided by the audit team after consideration of all the audit findings.*
Audit criteria	*The set of policies, procedures, or requirements determined as a reference.*
Audit evidence	The records, statements of fact, or other information relevant to the agreed-upon criteria and that can be crosschecked.
Audit findings	The results of the evaluation of collected audit evidence against audit criteria.
Audit plan	The description of the activities and arrangements for an audit.
Audit scope	The extent and boundaries of an audit.
Auditee	Organization being audited.
Auditor (quality)	Person qualified to perform quality audits.

B

Baseline	A set of measurements that establishes the status of a system or other item as of a given date. Used to provide a common denominator and starting point for later measurements and comparisons.

Batch	A definite quantity of product or material produced under same conditions.
Benchmark data	The results of an investigation to determine how competitors and/or best-in-class companies achieve their level of performance.
Benchmarking	A continuous process of measurement of products, services, and work processes against those recognized as industry leaders.
Best practices	Standard, published operating methods found to produce the best performance and results in a given industry or organization.
Beta test	*A software version released to a limited population of users for functionality and bug test evaluation before the final release to the general user base.*
Bill of material (BOM)	A structured list of the items used in making a parent assembly that reflects the actual production process in terms of timing and quantities consumed. It is constructed in conjunction with the *routing*, which describes the individual production steps and rates used. A BOM may optionally include information relating to back-flushing, use of alternate and optional components, ties between components and the operations that use them, and other data. BOMs are used by the *MRP*s function to calculate component requirements when given a parent demand and in building product costs.
Bimodal Distribution	A statistical distribution having two modes—indicating a mixing of two populations such as different shifts, machines, methods, or workers.

BS	British standard.
Bulk material	Products that do not have the characteristics of formed parts when received but become part of the product during the manufacturing process.

C

CA	Corrective action.
CAPA	Corrective action and preventive action.
Capability	The total range of inherent variation in a stable process.
Calibration	Determination of the experimental relationship between the quantity being measured and the output of the device that measures it; through a recognized standard of measurement.
CAR	Corrective action request.
Cell	A manufacturing layout that arranges workstations performing the different functions required to produce a product or subassembly in the same, often U-shaped area, rather that arranging machines by similar functions. Operators are usually trained to perform and complete all cell-manufacturing functions.
CE mark	European Union product-safety certification symbol: Œ.
CEN	European Committee for Standardization.

Certificate of compliance	A document signed by an authorized party affirming that the supplier of a product or service has met the requirements of the relevant *specifications*, contract, or regulation.
Closed-loop MRP	The system extending the original single function of material requirements planning (MRP) by including higher-level, long-term production planning, master production scheduling (MPS), capacity requirements planning (CRP), production control, and purchasing. Where the original MRP's function strictly generated a materials plan by exploding bills of material, closed-loop MRP creates feedback and interaction by measuring the proposed material plan against longer-term production and sales goals, verifying that capacity is available to complete the proposed production, and incorporating date and quantity changes to original plans required by vendors or the production floor.
Common cause	A source of *variation* that is always present as part of the random variation inherent in the *process* itself. Its origin can usually be traced to an element of the system that only management can correct.
Compliance	An affirmative indication or judgment that the **supplier** of a product or service has met the requirements of the relevant *specifications*, contract, or regulation; also the state of meeting regulatory requirements.
Component	Any raw material, substance, piece, part, software, firmware, labeling, or assembly that is intended to be included as part of the finished, packaged, and labeled device.

Concession	Permission to use or release a *product* that does not conform to specified *requirements*. Also called a *Waiver*.
Conformance	An affirmative indication or judgment that a product or service has met the requirements of the relevant *specifications*, contract, or regulation; also the state of meeting the requirements.
Continuous improvement	The never-ending pursuit of waste elimination by creating a better workplace, better products, and greater value to society.
Control element	Any specific process variable that must be controlled. The measurement of a control element indicates whether the process is operating under stable conditions.
Core competencies	Skills that provide the main competitive differentiation and overall base of knowledge for an organization. They may be the result of enhanced performance in a given department, such as engineering or marketing, or cross-functional such as the ability of a company to efficiently assemble the multiple skill sets needed to bid and complete large projects. Systems and departments that do not form a core competency are often candidates for outsourcing (e.g., a firm with an exceptional semiconductor design engine).
Corrective action plan	A plan for correcting a process or part quality issue.
Cost of poor quality	Costs associated with supplying a poor-quality product. Categories of cost include internal and external failure costs.

Cost of quality	Costs that would be eliminated if quality were perfect, which often include incoming raw material inspection, corrective engineering change orders, scrap, in-process control systems, downtime, material and labor rework charges, quality personnel labor costs, field service repair personnel, returned goods processing, customer warranty claims, and many others.
Cp	Process capability index measuring the ratio between actual spread (upper control limit minus lower control limit) divided by allowable or expected spread as measured by standard deviation.
Cross-functional	An activity, system, or team that contains more than one functional area within an organization and may involve balancing conflicting objectives.
Current Good Manufacturing Practices (cGMP)	Regulations as specified by the U.S. FDA or other regulatory body that describe the methods, equipment, and control procedures required for food processing, medical device manufacturing, and related industries.
D	
Dashboard	A set of metrics, usually not more than five or six, that provides an "at-a-glance" summary of a Six Sigma project's status. Every participant in a Six Sigma deployment—from the CEO to a factory floor worker—should have his or her own dashboard with function- and level-appropriate data summaries.

Data	Factual information used as a basis for reasoning, discussion, or calculation; often refers to quantitative information.
Defect	No fulfillment of a *requirement* related to an intended or specified use.
Design input	The physical and performance requirements of a device that are used as a basis for device design.
Design of experiment	Planning and conducting experiments and evaluating the results. The outcome of a design of experiment includes a mathematical equation predicting the interaction of the factors influencing a process and the relevant output characteristics of the process.
Design review	A documented, comprehensive, systematic examination of a design to evaluate the adequacy of the design requirements to evaluate the *capability* of the design to meet these requirements and identify problems.
Design validation	Testing to ensure that product conforms to defined user needs and/or requirements. Design *validation* follows successful *design verification* and is normally performed on the final product under defined operating conditions. Multiple validations may be performed if there are different intended uses.

Design verification	Testing to ensure that all design outputs meet design input requirements. Design verification may include activities such as: • Design review • Performing alternate calculations • Understanding tests and demonstrations Review of design stage documents before release.
Deviation	To depart from specified requirements, methods, or work instructions.
DFMEA	Design failure mode and effect analysis.
E	
EN	European standard.
End user	The final consumer of a product or service that ultimately determines its acceptability.
Engineering change order (ECO)	A formal document that has been signed off on by the affected departments and authorizes product definition changes to a drawing, bill of material, or routing. It often ties to system planning, scheduling, and cost functions by specifying an affectivity date for the items included.
Engineering change request	A document requesting a revision or change to a product or process that optimally includes the reason, urgency level, items and processes affected, and cost/benefit of the change. Signoff by a review board is normally required before the change is enacted.
EQS	European Committee for *Quality System* Assessment and

F	
First-article inspection	The analysis of the first item manufactured in a production run to verify correct setup and process alignment.
Fishbone diagram	A systematic analysis tool that organizes the effects of a problem and its possible causes in a graphical display that often resembles the skeleton of a fish. Developed by Dr. Kaoru Ishikawa, it is sometimes referred to as an Ishikawa diagram.
Gap analysis	Comparison to the best in the business in a specified quality area.
FIFO	First in first out inventory-management system.
I, J, K, L, M	
Impact analysis	The process of determining the organizational costs and benefits of a proposed alternative.
Just-in-time (JIT)	A manufacturing and inventory management philosophy that seeks to effectively manage resources and improve organizational effectiveness by identifying and eliminating sources of waste (anything that does not add to the customer's perception of value). Among other areas, it focuses on the reduction of lead times, small lot sizes, flexible production facilities and workforces, elimination of quality defects, and the reduction of inventory levels to as close to zero as possible. Inventory is seen in the JIT philosophy as not necessarily an asset, but as an unnecessary cost and potential liability that lengthens lead times, increases the chance for obsolescence, and hides inefficient processes and systems. It also emphasizes group and partner involvement in design, manufacturing, and logistics.

Kaizen	Taken from the Japanese words kai and zen, where kai means change and zen means good. The popular meaning is continual improvement of all areas of a company and not just quality. A business philosophy of continuous cost reduction, reduced quality problems, and delivery time reduction through rapid, team-based improvement activity.
Kanban	A Just-in-Time technique developed in Japan at the Toyota Corporation in which a work center or department uses a visible card, token, or other signal (kanban) to pull material from a feeder work center or supply location. It often uses a standard container with a card attached that is pulled when the container is moved by the using work center; after removal the card is used by the feeder work center as authorization for more production. A basic premise is that no production takes place until authorized by the using department. A two-card system uses both a production card, which authorizes the manufacture of a standard container, and a move card, which authorizes the transfer of a container from one work center to the next.
Key performance indicator (KPI)	Indicators used to provide measurements of the defined priority and key success factors of a project, process or Quality system.
Kitting	The process of pulling a set of component items from stock to group them for production or for movement to another area. Kitting is usually done for a specific production or sales order.

Manufacturing instructions	The detailed process parameters and operating data required for a specific production operation, which may include both basic production-rate data and detailed engineering specifications and notes.
Material	1) The raw materials and purchased components used in the production of other items. 2) The classification of any lower-level item, whether purchased or manufactured. A subassembly that has material, labor, and overhead content may be considered strictly as material in the context of being used in an upper-level item.
Material review board (MRB)	A cross-functional group that reviews production or purchased items on hold due to usability concerns and determines their disposition, which may include rework, scrap, or returning to the vendor.
Metrics	A standard or basis of measurement, such as cost, size, volume, etc.
P, Q, R, S	
Process	The combination of people, machine and equipment, raw materials, methods, and environment that produces a given product or service.
Process flow	Sequence of steps that add value to outputs of a previous task to produce a final product or services.
Process map	Sequential representation of processes and tasks between functions.

QSIT	Quality system inspection techniques. A technique used by FDA auditors to audit quality systems.
QSR	Quality system requirements.
Quality	Degree to which a set of inherent (existing) characteristics fulfils *requirements*. Meeting expectation and requirements, stated and unstated, of the customer.
Quality assurance	The set of activities that specifies acceptable material and process parameters and measures actual performance in meeting defined quality standards. When used in reference to a department—quality assurance (QA) or quality control (QC)—it often indicates that responsibility for meeting quality standards has been delegated to that department and is not an assumed function of other company operations.
Quality audit	(Also quality assessment, or conformity assessment) A systematic and independent examination and evaluation to determine whether quality activities and results comply with planned arrangements and whether these arrangements are implemented effectively and are suitable to achieve objectives.
Quality control	The operational techniques and the activities used to fulfill requirements of quality. Part of quality management focused on fulfilling quality *requirements*.
Quality Engineering	The branch of engineering that deals with the principles and practice of product and service quality assurance and control.

Quality management	The aspect of the overall business management function that determines and implements the quality policy.
Quality management system	Management system to direct and control an organization with regard to quality.
Quality manual	Document specifying the quality management system of an organization.
Quality plan	Document specifying which *procedures* and associated resources shall be applied by whom and when to a specific *project, product, process,* or contract.
Quality policy	The overall intentions and direction of an organization as regards quality as formally expressed by top management.
Return on investment (ROI)	The ratio of operating income divided by total assets employed that indicates the relative operating efficiency of an organization.
Return to vendor (RTV)	Purchased material determined to be unacceptable by receiving inspection or during the production process and designated for return to the supplier for credit or replacement.
Returned goods authorization (RGA)	The approval of a customer product return for credit, rework, or repair that normally has a unique identifier, specifies the products involved and sometimes the original shipment information, and serves as the authorization for processing at the receiving location.

Risk analysis	The identification of possible risks, assessment of their likelihood and impact, and creation of methods to avoid or reduce them.
Root cause	The most basic underlying reason for an event or condition. The root cause is where action must be taken to prevent recurrence.
Root-cause analysis	A process improvement and error- or defect-prevention tool that examines the individual processes within a system, identifies the control or decision points, and uses a series of why questions to determine the reasons for variations in the process paths.
SCAR	Supplier corrective action request.
Supplier	An internal or external organization that provides a product or a service to a customer.
System	A set of processes that work together as a unit to produce a collective result. A system comprises processes that are dependent on each other.
Validation	Proof through objective evidence that a process consistently performs to produce predetermined results.
Variance	The difference between a standard or expected value and the actual result; often characterized as favorable or unfavorable.
Variation	The inevitable differences among individual outputs of a *process*. The sources of variation can be grouped into two major classes: common and *special causes*.

Verification	The act of reviewing, *inspecting*, *testing*, checking, auditing, or otherwise establishing and documenting whether items, *processes*, services, or documents *conform* to specified *requirements*.
Voice of the customer (VOC)	A systematic, institutionalized approach for eliciting and analyzing customers' requirements. In Six Sigma and other quality improvement programs, the identification and prioritization of true customer needs and requirements through the use of focus groups, interviews, and other methods.
Voice of the process	Statistical data that is fed back to the people in the process to make decisions about the process stability and/or capability as a tool for continual improvement.
Zero defects	A quality philosophy based on the idea that a level of perfect quality, as in zero defects, is achievable and should be a company-wide goal. It emphasizes the examination of all factors that lead to quality problems

This is a partial list of terms used to define parts of the Quality management system. The vocabulary you choose should be dependent on the culture of your organization, and the product your organization manufactures. However, the baseline for your vocabulary should be the definitions used by the FDA.

CHAPTER ELEVEN
HOW THE FDA AUDITS QUALITY SYSTEMS

FDA auditors follow the QSIT (quality system inspection technique) when they audit quality management systems. The technique is based on the following principles:
- The quality system is designed, implemented, owned, and managed by management
- Management is responsible for the health of the quality system
- All problems in the quality system can be tied to management
- There are seven quality management subsystems in a given quality system (five for pharmaceutical companies)
- Management controls and monitors the other six quality subsystems

ORDER OF THE AUDIT

The FDA quality audits are systemic. The auditor starts with management controls and ends with management control. Here is the order in which your quality subsystems will be audited:

1. **Management controls**
    High on the priority list of this quality subsystem are management review, management review meeting records, and CAPA escalations.

2. **Design controls**

   Design controls will include change control, design transfer, and design validation.

3. **CAPA**

   Auditors love this quality subsystem because of its importance in the quality system. High on the list will be the so-called "closed-loop" corrective action and preventive action. In other words, all phases of your CAPA will be looked at. I strongly advice all my clients to be aware of CAPA requirements in 21CFR 820.100(J).

4. **Production and process controls**

   Next to CAPA and management controls this is the most audited quality subsystem. Items to be audited will include batch records, equipment maintenance records, training records, calibration records, master validation plans, validation reports, validation protocols, work instructions, and standard operating procedures.

5. **Management controls**

   An FDA audit usually starts with management controls and ends with management controls. Auditors do this for two reasons: First, auditing the management controls subsystem first establishes linkages between quality subsystem failures to management controls; the second reason is to inform the management representative with executive authority about any of the audit findings or nonconformities that may be found during the audit.

THE AUDIT APPROACH

To audit a quality system, FDA auditors follow what is usually referred to as the **"top-down"** approach. The top-down approach involves the following:

- Obtaining a picture of the entire quality system by interviewing the management representative or designee. In most cases the management representative is the vice president of quality.

MANAGEMENT CONTROLS
- Review of the quality policy
- Review of the organizational structure
- Review of defined functional areas, with roles and responsibilities
- Review of management review standard operating procedure (SOP)
- Review of management review records
- Review of audit procedures and schedules
- Review of audit records

DESIGN CONTROLS
- Review of design controls, including elements from design input to design transfer, verification, design review, and process validation
- Review of design change control
- Review of a selected project with emphasis on the design plan and design procedure
- Review of design validation data
- Review of software validation
- Review of any design changes, reviews, and risk analysis and hazard analysis methodology including any FMEAs, or FTAs
- Review of design-transfer methodology

CAPA
- Review of the CAPA standard operating procedure
- Review of failure analysis methodology from discovery to closure
- Review of CAPA records
- Review of sources of quality problems
- Review of containment methodology
- Review of trend analysis methodology
- Review of statistical methods used
- Review of data from failure analysis
- Review of validated or verified solutions prior to implementation
- Review of actions taken and decisions made
- Review of the documentation system of all action taken
- Review of the information dissemination system to management with executive authority and management review.
- Review of timeliness for information dissemination to management review

- Review of methods for trend analysis
- Review and determination of whether the depth or degree of investigation is sufficient for a selected problem, or potential problem.
- Review of nonconforming product records

FOR MEDICAL DEVICE ONLY:
- Review and verification of MDR procedures and files.
- Review of the enforcement and effectiveness of the MDR procedure
- Review of MDR event files
- Review of file for non-reportable corrections and removals.
- Review of medical device tracking standard operating procedure

PRODUCTION AND PROCESS CONTROLS

Next to CAPA and management controls, this is one quality subsystem that is guaranteed to be audited. The focus of the audit is usually the following elements:
- Process flow
- Process parameters and control limits
- Process standard operating procedures or work instructions
- In-process acceptance activities
- Finished product acceptance activities
- Environmental controls
- Nonconformance material handling
- Equipment calibration
- Equipment maintenance
- Process validation or verification
- Software validation (for processes that are controlled by software)
- Personnel training and qualifications
- Sterilization process controls

SAMPLE SIZE SELECTION

The auditor chooses sample sizes for records, standard operating procedures, or work instructions to review based on the risk posed by the product to the public. In most cases it is either the 95/95 confidence level or 99/99 confidence level. Usually the sequences of events are:
- Selection of confidence level to use
- Selection of sample size
- Review of sample documents selected

- Record of findings

The final stage is usually the final meeting with the management representative or designee to go over audit findings.

Appendix A
QUALITY SYSTEM WARNING LETTERS

The following are samples of warning letters from the FDA to different organizations. This information is in the public domain on the FDA website. The information is provided here to give the reader of this book a flavor of issues the FDA deems essential for a well-designed quality management system that meets the quality System Requirements (QSR):

ISSUE 1: CAPA

-----Our investigators found significant deviations from requirements set forth in the quality system regulation at Title 21 code of Federal Regulations (21CFR); Part 820. These deviations include but are not limited to the following:

(a) Failure to establish and maintain an adequate corrective and preventive action procedure that ensures identification of actions needed to correct and prevent the recurrence of nonconforming products and other quality problems, as required by 21CFR 820.100(a)(3). For example-------

(b) Failure to document the implementation of corrective and preventive actions, as required by 21 CFR 820.100(b). For example----------

(c) Failure for your organization to establish procedures to completely address identification, documentation, evaluation, segregation, disposition, and investigation of nonconforming products as required by 21 CFR 820.90(a). For example--------------------

(d) Failure to establish and maintain procedures for implementing corrective and preventive actions, including procedures for analyzing processes, work operations, concessions, quality audit reports, quality records, service records, complaints, returned products, or other quality problems, as required by 21 CFR 820.100(a)(1). For example------------------

(e) Failure to develop, maintain, and implement written MDR procedures, as required by 21 CFR 803.17. For example your complaint procedure---------

(f) Failure to thoroughly investigate or maintain a written record of the investigation of any unexplained discrepancy or the failure of a batch or any of its components to meet any of its specifications, whether or not the batch has been distributed, and the failure to extend the investigation to other batches of the same drug product and other drug products that may have been associated with the specific failure or discrepancy as required by 21 CFR 211.192.

(g) Failure to adequately establish and maintain procedures for implementing corrective and preventive action, as required by 21 CFR 820.100. Specifically, your CAPA procedure does not describe how you will investigate quality problems other than those identified in complaints.

(h) Failure to evaluate and review complaints to determine if an investigation is necessary, as required by 21 CFR 820.198(b). For example------------

ISSUE 2: MANAGEMENT CONTROLS

--------"At the close of the inspection you were issued a Form FDA-483, a list of inspectional observations that identified a number of violations, including, but not limited to:"

(a) Failure to establish procedures for quality audits and conduct such audits to ensure that the quality system is in compliance with the established quality system requirement, as required by 21 CFR820.22.For example----

(b) Management with executive responsibility has failed to ensure that an adequate quality system has been fully implemented and maintained at all levels of your organization, as required by 21CFR 820.20(c). No management reviews have been conducted prior to FDA's most recent inspection of your firm.

(c) Failure to assure that management with executive responsibility reviews the suitability and effectiveness of the quality system at defined intervals and with sufficiency according to established procedures to ensure that the quality system satisfies the requirements of this part and the manufacturer's established quality policy and objectives as required by 21CFR 820.20(C). For example--------------

(d) Failure of the management with executive responsibility to ensure that an adequate and effective quality system has been fully implemented and maintained at all levels of the organization, as required by 21 CFR 829.20. For example-----------------

(e) Failure to establish and maintain adequate management review procedures and conduct adequate management reviews to meet the requirements of the quality system regulation and manufacturer's established quality policy and objectives, as required by 21CFR 820.22 (C). Your firm's management failed to review all quality sources and take appropriate corrective actions to address various quality issues or document their adequate justification for not taking corrective action. For example-------------

(f) Failure to identify the actions needed to correct and prevent recurrence of nonconforming product and other quality problems, as required by 21CFR 820.100(a) (3). For example--------------

(g) During inspection of your firm our investigators found significant observations in the operation of your firm's quality control unit, and as a result there is no assurance that many drug products manufactured and released into interstate commerce by your firm have the identity, strength, quality, and purity that they purport to possess.

(h) Failure to document training and ensure that all personnel are trained to adequately perform their assigned responsibilities, as required by 21CFR 820.25(b).

(i) Failure to establish and maintain an adequate organizational structure to ensure that devices are designed and produced in accordance with established quality system requirements as required by 21 CFR 820.20(b). For example, your firm has no management representative with executive responsibilities to oversee the quality system.

(j) Failure to establish and maintain procedures for quality audits and conduct quality audits to assure that the quality system is in compliance with established quality system requirements and to determine the effectiveness of the quality system, as required by 21CFR 820.22.

ISSUE 3: PRODUCTION AND PROCESS CONTROLS

(a) Our inspection revealed that devices are adulterated within the meaning of section 501(h) of the act, in that methods used are not in conformity with current Good Manufacturing Practices requirements of the quality system regulations. Significant violations include but are not limited to failure to establish and maintain procedures for the identification, documentation, validation, or, where appropriate, verification, review, and approval of process changes before implementation. For example-------------------

(b) Failure to establish and maintain procedures for finished device acceptance to ensure that each production run, lot, or batch of finished devices meet acceptance criteria, as required by 21CFR 820.80(d). For example your firm does not have any written final inspection operating procedure for xxxx.

(c) Failure to establish and maintain procedures to prevent contamination of equipment or product by substances that could reasonably be expected to have an adverse effect on product quality, as required by 21CFR 820.70(e).

(d) Failure to establish and maintain procedures to adequately control environmental conditions, as required by 21 CFR 820.70(C). Specifically, temperature conditions within the aseptic-processing area are not being documented to ensure that such conditions are consistently within established specifications.

(e) Failure to ensure that all equipment used in manufacturing meet specifications and is appropriately designed, constructed, placed, and installed to facilitate maintenance, adjustment, cleaning, and use as required by 21CFR 820.70(g).

(f) Failure to document maintenance activities, including the date and individuals performing the activities, as required by 21CFR 820.70(g) (1). Specifically------------

(g) There are no procedures indicating the amount of time finished products are allowed to remain stored in trailers before finding a location in the warehouse for storage.

ISSUE 4: DESIGN CONTROLS

(a) Failure to establish and maintain a design history file to demonstrate that the design was developed in accordance with the approved design plan and design requirements of the quality system regulation specified in 21CFR 820.30(J)

(b) Failure to establish and maintain procedures to ensure that the device history records (DHRRS) for each batch, lot, or unit are maintained to demonstrate that the device is manufactured in accordance with the device master record (DMR) and the established quality system requirements of 21CFR part 820, as required by 21CFR 820.184.

(c) Failure to establish and maintain design plans that describe or reference the design and development activities and identify the interfaces with other groups or activities, as required by 21CFR 820.30(b). Specifically -----------------

(d) Failure to establish and maintain procedures for verifying the device design that confirm that the design output meets the design input requirements as required by 21CFR 820.30(f).

(e) Failure to establish and maintain procedures to ensure that the device design is correctly translated into production specifications, as required by 21CFR 820.30(h). Specifically-- -----------

(f) Failure to ensure that formal documented reviews of the design results are planned and conducted at appropriate stages of the device's design development as require by 21CFR820.30(e). Specifically----------

Appendix B
BIBLIOGRAPHY

FDA

Compliance Program Guidance Manual. *Transmittal 95-30.* May 4, 1995.

Guide to Inspection of Quality Systems (QSIT). August 1, 1999.

Inspection of Medical Device Manufacturers. *Compliance Program 7382.80, FDA Compliance Program Guidance Manual.* May 4, 1995.

Medical Device Quality System Manual: *A Small Entity Compliance Guide.* HHS Pub. No. 84-4191. April 1994.

Parts 210 and 211 cGMP in Manufacturing, Processing, Packing, or Holding of Drugs and Finished Pharmaceuticals.

21CFR Part 1271. Human Cells, Tissues, and Cellular Therapy and Tissue-based Products.

21CFR Parts 600 and 606. Blood Products and Biologics.

21CFR Part 820.00. Quality Systems Requirements.

ISO

Quality Management Systems: Requirements. ISO 9001:200.

Quality Systems: Medical Devices Supplementary Requirements to ISO 9001: 13485, 1995.

ISO 13485: 2003(E)

OTHER
CA/CSA ISO 13485:2003, Jan 2003

This is a little story about four people named **SOMEBODY, EVERYBODY, ANYBODY, and NOBODY.** There was an important job to be done, and **EVERYBODY** thought that **SOMEBODY** would do it. As it turns out, **NOBODY** did it, and **SOMEBODY** was ticked off because it was **EVERYBODY'S** job, and **ANYBODY** could have done it.

QSi (LLC) is a member of the Silicon Valley (San Jose) chamber of commerce and

a member of the **San Jose B**etter **B**usiness **B**ureau.

Quality is everybody's job!™

QSi **consultants**
www.qualitysystemsinternational.net
(408) 266-3978.

Lightning Source UK Ltd.
Milton Keynes UK
175656UK00001B/54/P